THE ECONOMIC HISTORY
OF WORLD POPULATION

THE ECONOMIC HISTORY
OF WORLD POPULATION

CARLO M. CIPOLLA
Professor of Economic History,
University of California

THE HARVESTER PRESS · SUSSEX

BARNES AND NOBLE BOOKS · NEW YORK

This edition first published in 1978 by
THE HARVESTER PRESS LIMITED
Publisher: John Spiers
2 Stanford Terrace
Hassocks, Nr Brighton
Sussex, England
and published in the U.S.A. 1978 by
HARPER & ROW PUBLISHERS, INC.,
BARNES & NOBLE IMPORT DIVISION
10 East 53rd Street, New York 10022

The Economic History of World Population
This edition first published in 1978
by The Harvester Press Limited
and by Barnes & Noble
By agreement with Penguin

First published in paperback 1962
by Penguin Books
Seventh edition 1978 in paperback

© Carlo Cipolla, 1962, 1964, 1965, 1967, 1970,
1974, 1978

British Library Cataloguing in Publication Data

Cipolla, Carlo Maria
    The economic history of world population – 7th ed.
    1. Population
    I. Title
    301.32   HB851
ISBN 0–85527–735–5

Barnes & Noble
ISBN 0–06–491138–1

Printed and bound in Great Britain by
Redwood Burn Limited, Trowbridge & Esher

*Manlio, dilectissimo fratri,
probo viro necnon
medico praeclaro,
in omni parte humanitatis
versato*

D.D.D.

Contents

List of Text Figures

List of Tables

Preface to the First Edition

FAST and cheap transportation has been one of the main products of the Industrial Revolution. Distances have been shortened at an astonishing pace. Day by day the world seems smaller and smaller and societies that for millennia practically ignored each other are suddenly put in contact –or in conflict. In our dealings, in politics as in economics, in health organization as in military strategy, a new point of view is forced upon us. At some time in the past people had to move from an urban or regional point of view to a national one. Today we have to adjust ourselves and our ways of thinking to a *global* point of view. As Bertrand Russell wrote, 'The world has become one not only for the astronomer but for the ordinary citizen.'

This book attempts to describe from a global point of view the development of mankind in its material endeavour: its growth in numbers and levels of living. From the same global point of view, I have tried to touch upon some of the alarming problems that mankind is facing today: the population explosion, the growing need for energy resources, the diffusion of technical knowledge, and the role of education in an industrial society.

Writing this book has been a most ambitious task; but I could count on the help of learned friends and colleagues whom I exploited with indecent pertinacity. Among the more illustrious victims I must remember Miss Phyllis Deane, Gregory Grossman, Alexander Gershenkron, Harvey Leibenstein, Martin Hofbaum, and Henry Rosovsky. Adam Pepelasis and George Richardson read the manuscript in its entirety and gave me all kinds of valuable criticisms and suggestions. My friends John Guthrie and John Scott, and my students Victoria Chick, Elizabeth Conner, Walter Abbott, Harold Jackson, and Hans Palmer helped me with linguistic problems. My secretary Franca Zennaro is firmly convinced that the age of slavery is not yet over. To all of them I want to express my gratitude while reassuring them with the statement that no one of them is to be held responsible for any of the views expressed in this book.

Berkeley, California, October 1960

PREFACE TO THE THIRD EDITION

I wish to extend my thanks to my friends Lennart Jorberg and V. Paretti who kindly assisted me in bringing up to date some of the statistics published in this book.

Pavia, Italy, July 1965

PREFACE TO THE FIFTH EDITION

This fifth edition has been thoroughly revised and brought up to date. I wish to thank Miss Mary Bergen, Mr. W. Chamberlain, Professor Kwang-chih Chang, and Professor Gregory Grossman for their advice and their help.

Berkeley, California, Summer 1969

PREFACE TO THE SIXTH EDITION

World population keeps growing, our knowledge about historic and prehistoric times keeps expanding, mankind is plagued by an ever increasing number of seemingly intractable problems. To write this book was surely an easier task than to keep it up to date and save it from the obsolescence which threatens us and things around us in this hallucinatingly changing world.

Eugene, Oregon, Summer 1972

Acknowledgements

I AM indebted to many publishers and authors for permission to quote passages and reprint figures. In particular I have to acknowledge my grateful indebtedness to the following:

Abelard-Schuman Ltd of London for permission to quote a passage from *Man the Maker* by R. J. Forbes (London–New York, 1958); Doubleday & Co. of New York for granting me permission to quote a passage from *Back of History* by W. Howells (New York, 1954); Harper & Brothers of New York for permission to quote a passage from the *Adventures with the Missing Link* by R. A. Dart (New York, 1959); George G. Harrap & Co. of London and the Indiana University Press for granting me permission to reproduce figure 16 and figure 75 from *Power and Production* (*Energy for Man* in the American edition) by H. Thirring; Professor Dudley Kirk for permission to reproduce figure 46 from his book *Europe's Population in the Interwar Years* (New York, 1946); the Viking Press of New York for permission to quote a passage from *The Challenge of Man's Future* by H. Brown (New York, 1954).

15

CHAPTER 1

The Two Revolutions

THERE are nine major planets in the solar system. One of them is the earth. It is one of the nearest to the sun, one of the smallest in diameter, and one of the most dense, with perhaps the highest density of all.

The earth is covered with a thin film of matter called life. 'The film is exceedingly thin, so thin that its weight can scarcely be more than one-billionth [1000 millionth] that of the planet which supports it. . . . [It is] so insignificant in size that it would be detectable only with the greatest difficulty by beings on other planets, and would certainly be unnoticeable to observers elsewhere in our galaxy. . . . It is insubstantial, flaccid, and sensitive in the extreme so that a slight cosmic ripple would quickly bring destruction. Yet, in an ever-changing way, the envelope of living things has continued to exist for the greatest part of the earth's history.'[1]

'Man' is part of this thin, living envelope. But he made a very late appearance. Vermes were already on the earth almost 450 million years ago, jawless fishes 400 million years, scorpions 350 million years, bony fishes 300 million years, amphibia 270 million years, reptilia 250 million years, winged insects 225 million years, grasshoppers 215 million years, birds 140 million years, marsupials 80 million years.[2] Man appeared in his present form (*homo sapiens*) some half a million years ago. He appeared when many other species had already died out and when all other species that exist today had already been on earth for a long, long time.

1. Brown, 1954, p. 3. (See Bibliography for details of books mentioned in footnotes.)
2. Zeuner, 1958, p. 365.

THE AGRICULTURAL REVOLUTION

For thousands of years, man lived as a predatory animal. Hunting, fishing, gathering wild fruits, and killing and eating other men remained for a very long time the only ways by which man could secure for himself the necessary means of subsistence. As a most ancient Sumerian text forcibly evoked, 'when the human species appeared, it did not know bread nor cloth. Man walked on hands and feet. He ate grass with the mouth as animals do, and he drank the water of the stream.'[3] In the course of time, particular skills and techniques were invented and developed – the cutting of stones, the making of special weapons, the building of transport devices – but everything remained in the general framework of a predatory economy. New skills and innovations merely helped to increase man's efficiency in hunting, fishing, and killing. 'Man lived as a really primitive hunter and gatherer of wild fruits and vegetables for all but one per cent of his known existence.'[4]

Only recently – somewhere, somehow – the first great economic revolution occurred: the discovery of agriculture and the domestication of animals.

In the Near East incipient cultivation and domestication developed after 10,000 B.C.[5] It is customary now to distinguish between two major phases, the Proto-Neolithic phase covering approximately the period 9000 to 7000 B.C. and the Neolithic phase covering approximately the period 7000 to 5500 B.C. In terms of economy, the Proto-Neolithic is the phase in which there are indications that the Neolithic Revolution from food-gathering to food-production was under way. By Neolithic times farming and stock breeding were well

3. Quoted by Pirenne, 1950, Vol. 1, p. 4.
4. Howells, 1959, p. 143.
5. For all that follows cf. Braidwood and Willey, 1962, and Mellaart, 1965.

established and the basic level of the effective village farming community had been achieved. The following are some of the major findings. Bones of domesticated sheep appeared in the upper portion of layer B in the cave of Shanidar in the foothills of the Zagros Mountains. A radiocarbon determination dated the remains at about 8500 B.C. At about the same date there were people who inhabited open stations at Karim Shahir and Zawi Chemi Shanidar and they too had domesticated sheep.[6] Excavations in the inward slopes of the Zagros mountain crescent provided evidence of a village farm community at Jarmo in Iraq. The village was seemingly inhabited between 7000 and 6500 B.C.[7] The people of Jarmo domesticated goats and grew barley and two different kinds of wheat.[8]

In the Dead Sea Valley of Palestine, excavations in the Jericho oasis laid bare the spectacular remains of a pre-pottery, early Neolithic settlement. The settlement was surrounded by a solid, free standing stone wall 6 feet 6 inches wide, rising at some points to a height of 12 feet and flanked on the inner side by a circular tower still standing about 30 feet high. According to radiocarbon determinations the village developed after 8000 B.C. The tower and defences date back to about 7000 B.C.[9]

On the Anatolian Plateau, at Hacilar, the remains of a Neolithic site have been dated by radiocarbon at about 7000 B.C. About five hundred years later a large Neolithic city was flourishing at Çatal Hüyük.[10]

Archaeological research in South-West Asia is progressing at a very rapid pace, and the printed word becomes rapidly

6. Mellaart, 1965, p. 20; Clark, 1969, pp. 84–5.
7. Braidwood, 1961, p. 130.   8. ibid. p. 127.
9. Kenyon, 1960, p. 44. See also Kenyon, 1957, pp. 82–4, and Kenyon, 1959, p. 9.
10. Mellaart, 1967, pp. 15–66.

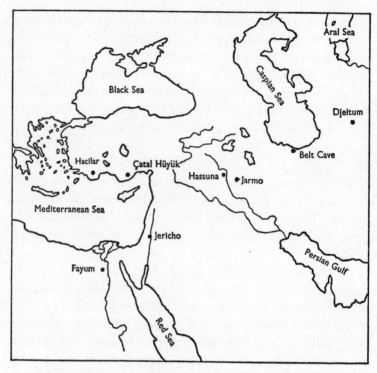

Fig. 1a. The sites of incipient agriculture in the Near East

obsolete.[11] It can be suggested, however, with a fair degree of assurance, that the foundations of settled life in the Old World were first laid in South-West Asia between the ninth and the seventh millennium B.C. This seemingly took place where prototypes of the earliest domesticated animals and plants existed in a wild state and where the concentration on particular species as sources of food was stimulated by the

11. The latest edition of Professor Clark's classical work on *World Prehistory* offers a most useful summary of recent archaeological discoveries and of the greatly increased volume of radiocarbon determinations.

20

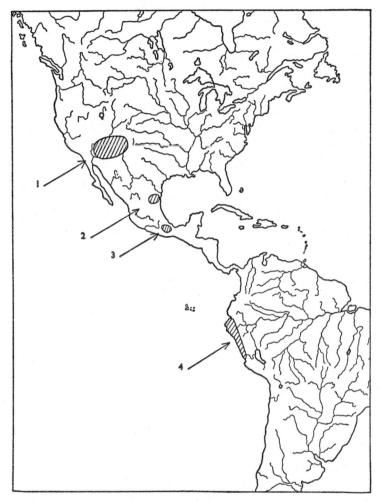

Fig. 1b. The areas of incipient agriculture on the American Continent

1. American Southwest
2. Southern Tamaulipas
3. Tehuacán Valley
4. Coastal Peru

ecological changes that marked the transition to Neothermal climate.[12]

On the American continent, four areas were investigated, namely the American Southwest, the Southern Tamaulipas area, the Tehuacán Valley and the Peruvian coast (see Fig. 1b). It seems that some kind of experimenting with plant domestication possibly took place in Mesoamerica between 7000 and 5000 B.C., but plant domestication of some importance effectively started after 5000 B.C. and along the Peruvian coast after 4000 B.C.[13] In comparison to the Near East story, American developments were not only later but also painfully slow. In the Tehuacán Valley plant domestication was well on the way during the period 5000 to 3500 B.C., but during the period 3500 to 2300 B.C. wild plants and game still represented about 70 per cent of the diet of the people, and effective food production and village agriculture did not appear until about 1500 B.C.[14] In Peru truly permanent villages did not appear until 750 B.C.[15] On the other hand, the Neolithic people of Mesoamerica had the merit of domesticating one of the most productive plants known to man. The oldest cobs of domesticated maize found north of Mexico City and in Mexico City itself date back to about 3000 B.C. Those found in the Tehuacán Valley have been dated at about 5000 B.C.[16] In Peru, Mesoamerican influence in the form of domesticated maize appeared at about 1400 B.C.[17]

What was the origin of the American developments? Was American agriculture introduced by Neolithic immigrants? Or was it the product of indigenous independent discovery? Scholars favour the second hypothesis.

12. Clark, 1969, p. 84.
13. MacNeish, 1964 and MacNeish, 1965.
14. MacNeish, 1964, pp. 20–28.   15. MacNeish, 1965, p. 89.
16. MacNeish, 1964, pp. 6–7.
17. Braidwood and Willey, 1962, p. 335.

What then about the East? There is no doubt that the Neolithic Revolution spread eastward from the Near East. Close to the shore of the Caspian Sea, around 5800 B.C., people living in the Belt Cave domesticated goats and sheep. By 5300 B.C. the cave was certainly inhabited by people who had begun to make pottery and to reap grain as well as to keep pigs and, later, cows.[18] By the end of the sixth millennium the Neolithic Revolution had reached Djeitum in Southern Turkmenia. Before 3500 B.C. it had reached Northern Baluchistan from Iran by way of Seistan and the Valley of the Helmand river.[19] About 2000 B.C. large parts of India outside Sind, the Punjab, Uttar Pradesh, Saurashtra – and even inside these regions – had a peasant-pastoral culture.[20] In Eastern Asia, China presents us with an unresolved problem, for here independent invention and importation from outside are equally plausible.[21] Was the Neolithic Revolution brought to Eastern Asia by Neolithic immigrants from the West? Or was there another independent nuclear area of the Revolution. The first well-defined Neolithic culture in China is the Yang-shao culture, named after the village in Western Honan. The Yang-shao culture seems to have emerged in the fifth millenium B.C., and possibly even earlier. In northwestern Thailand near the Burmese border, excavation at the Spirit Cave, sixty kilometres north of Mae Hongson brought to light domesticated plant material which can be dated about 7500 B.C. However, there is nothing definite as yet in the Spirit Cave finds that really challenges the Loess area of China as the first in the entire Far East to develop ordinary field agriculture.[22] In any case, more archaeological research

18. Coon, 1957, Chapter 4; 1958, p. 143.
19. Fairservis, 1956, p. 356; Masson, 1961, pp. 203–5; Clark, 1969, p. 208.
20. Sankalia, in Braidwood and Willey, 1962, p. 71.
21. Clark and Piggott, 1965, 156.
22. Chang, in Braidwood and Willey, 1962, pp. 179–80. Cf. also

will have to be carried out before we emerge from the realm of hazy hypotheses. In comparison with those of China, Japanese developments were relatively late. It was not until the third century B.C. that the basis of a peasant society was laid in Japan with the introduction of rice-cultivation and the beginning of the Yayoi culture.[23]

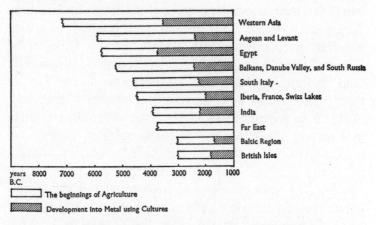

years 8000 7000 6000 5000 4000 3000 2000 1000
B.C.

☐ The beginnings of Agriculture

▨ Development into Metal using Cultures

Fig. 2. The diffusion of the Agricultural Revolution

To Africa and Europe the Neolithic Revolution came from the nuclear area in the Near East. In the Nile Valley, excavations along the shore of Lake Fayum laid bare remains of grain bins and silos dating from about 4300 B.C. Creeping south along the Nile, the Revolution reached Naqada around 3700 B.C., the Sudan (Shaheinab) possibly around 3200 B.C. and Kenya (Hyrax Hill) about 3000 B.C.[24] This southward movement was slowed down if not altogether stopped by the great swamps behind the headwaters of the Nile. Sub-

Fairservis, 1959, p. 139; Bishop, 1933, pp. 389–404; Chang, 1963; Chang, 1967; Ping-Ti Ho, 1969.   23. Clark, 1969, pp. 239–40.

24. Braidwood, 1961, p. 148; Cole, 1954, pp. 216–17; Clark, 1969, pp. 185 ff.

Saharan Africa seems never to have made any major contribution to food production or to any of the higher forms of the economy. In Western Africa, plant cultivation, and probably domestication, cannot have arrived at the proportions of effective food production until the beginning of the first millennium B.C.[25] In the meantime, from the nuclear area in the Near East, the Revolution spread into Europe. The Danube and the Mediterranean were the roads along which the new way of living invaded the West (Fig. 3a).[26] Between 4500 and 2000 B.C. an agricultural economy developed in the lands now known as the Balkans, Italy, France, Spain, Hungary, Switzerland, Germany, Holland, Denmark, the British Isles, and Scandinavia. By 1500 B.C. the last European stronghold of· the pure hunting economy was the zone of tundra and coniferous forest extending from the Norwegian coasts right across Northern Eurasia.[27]

In time the Agricultural Revolution spread all over the world. The hunters became 'marginal' in all senses of the word. 'Some were marginal in being remote and isolated literally at the world's ends: the Bushmen of South Africa, the natives of Australia, of the Andaman Islands in the Bay of Bengal and of the Tierra del Fuego at the bottom of South America. Most have been marginal in their resources and territory and have survived to this day because what they had no one else wanted, such as the last Bushman stronghold in the Kalahari Desert or the barren ground and arctic parts of Siberia and America.'[28]

25. Clark, in Braidwood and Willey, 1962, pp. 27 and 28.
26. cf. Hawkes and Woolley, 1963, pp. 238–54.
27. In general see Gordon Childe, 1958, especially Chapters 2 and 3; Piggott, 1954; Clark and Godwin, 1962, p. 21; Nougier, 1950; Bailloud, 1955; Zeuner, 1958, pp. 72–109; Quitta, 1967, p. 264, and the important Scandinavian bibliography quoted and summarized in Becker, 1955, pp. 749–66.   28. Howells, 1954, p. 120.

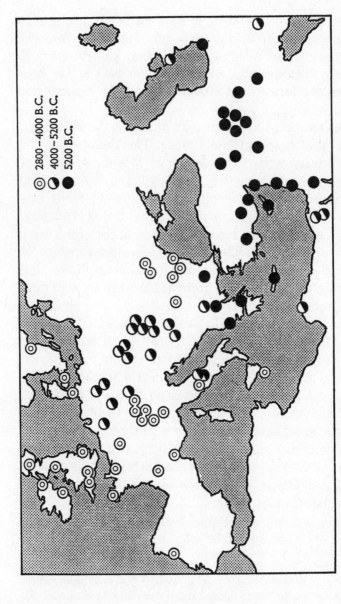

Fig. 3a. The spread of farming into Europe from South-West Asia charted by radiocarbon dates (from Clark, *World Prehistory*, 1969, p. 121, by permission of Cambridge University Press)

Legend:
◎ 2800 – 4000 B.C.
◖ 4000 – 5200 B.C.
● 5200 B.C.

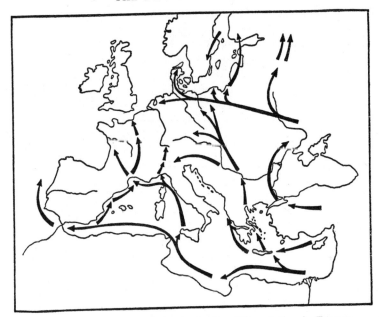

Fig. 3b. The diffusion of the Agricultural Revolution in Europe

By A.D. 1780 the hunting stage had long since been abandoned by nearly all mankind and the last strongholds of the hunters were being invaded by the triumphant farmers.

THE INDUSTRIAL REVOLUTION

Then, late in the eighteenth century, the second Revolution was born: the Industrial Revolution.[29] England was its cradle. Its diffusion was rapid. By 1850 it had penetrated into Belgium, France, Germany and the United States. By 1900 it had reached Sweden, Northern Italy and Russia. Japan, who had been so slow in importing the Agricultural Revo-

29. On the Industrial Revolution see among others Mantoux, 1928; Ashton, 1950; Deane, 1967; Hartwell, 1967; Landes, 1969; Mathias, 1969.

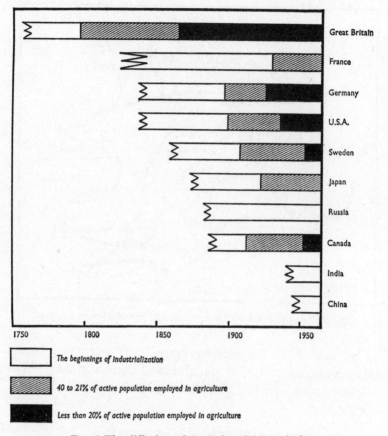

Fig. 4. The diffusion of the Industrial Revolution

lution from the Chinese mainland in the centuries B.C., was
the first Asian country to import the Industrial Revolution
in the twentieth century A.D. After 1950 the Industrial
Revolution spread into India, China, South America, and
Africa (Fig. 4).

Wherever the Industrial Revolution penetrated, it brought
into the entire structure of the society a general aggregate of
changes that made industry, instead of agriculture, the pre-

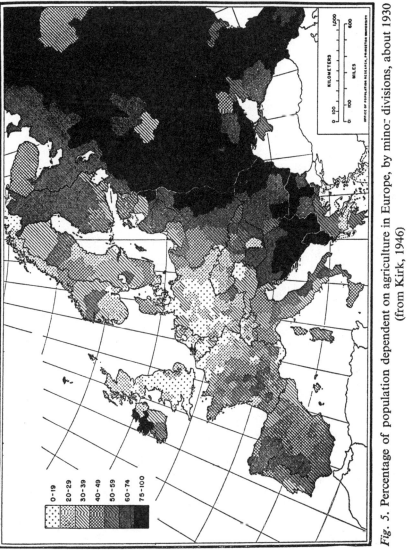

Fig. 5. Percentage of population dependent on agriculture in Europe, by minor divisions, about 1930 (from Kirk, 1946)

TABLE 1. *Percentage of active population employed in agriculture in selected countries, 1850, 1900, and 1950*

	About 1750	About 1850	About 1900	About 1950
AFRICA				
Algeria				81
Egypt			70	65
French Morocco				67
South Africa			60	33
Tunisia				70
AMERICA				
Argentina				25
Brazil				61
Canada			42	20
Mexico			70	61
U.S.A.		65	38	13
ASIA				
China				70
India				74
Japan			71	48
Malaya				65
Pakistan				80
Thailand				86
EUROPE				
Austria			60	33
Belgium		50	27	12
Czechoslovakia				38
Denmark		49	47	25
France	76	52	42	30
Germany			35	24
Great Britain	65	22	9	5
Greece				48
Ireland		48	45	40
Italy			60	42
Low Countries		44	31	20
Norway		65	41	26
Poland		82	77	57
Portugal			65	48
Spain		70	68	50
Sweden	75	65	54	21

	About 1750	About 1850	About 1900	About 1950
EUROPE—*cont.*				
Switzerland			35	16
Turkey				86
Yugoslavia				78
OCEANIA				
Australia			25	22
New Zealand			30	18
U.S.S.R.		90	85	56

TABLE 2. *Percentage of active population employed in agriculture by continents, 1900 and 1950*

	Percentage of the labour force employed in agriculture		
	1800	1900	1950
EUROPE		51	39
U.S.A.	80	38	13
LATIN AMERICA			54
SOUTH EAST ASIA		76	75
NORTH AFRICA			73
RUSSIA		80	45
WORLD	85	70	60

dominant productive sector of the society. The advance of the farmers was halted and indeed transformed into a rapid retreat. The proportion of the world's active population engaged in agriculture was most probably above 80 per cent in 1800. It was around 60 per cent in 1950 (see Tables 1 and 2) and it kept falling at a rapid pace. The day may not be too distant when the proportion of farmers in the world will be no larger than the proportion of hunters in the late eighteenth century.

Though industry now tends to predominate, we cannot say that the world tends to be populated by industrial workers. Most of the active members of an agricultural society are engaged in agricultural pursuits. In an industrial society a

31

much smaller proportion, 30 to 50 per cent, is actually employed in 'industry' – a good number of the rest are employed in a varied set of activities like government, banking, insurance, the liberal professions, and all sorts of service-producing business that economists and statisticians, for want of a better term, call the 'tertiary sector'.[30] Further development of 'automation' will probably further reduce the proportion of the active population actually engaged in 'industry'.[31]

WHAT SORT OF REVOLUTION?

Historians have too often over-emphasized the changes that constantly occur in history by labelling them 'Revolutions'. They detected an 'Urban Revolution' in early historic times, a 'Commercial Revolution' in eleventh-century Europe, a 'sort of Industrial Revolution' in eleventh-century Holland, and an 'Industrial Revolution' in thirteenth-century England. But from our point of view, at least, all these 'Revolutions' were scarcely revolutionary. They brought some changes, but they did not alter the fundamental economic character of the societies involved. When the first 'towns' appeared, the societies experiencing the new phenomenon continued to be fundamentally agricultural and the 'towns' were mere organs of a more complex agricultural world – often nothing more than collecting centres of agricultural rents. As Professor Frankfort has pointed out, 'The great divergence between city and countryside, between rural and urban life is, in the form in which we were familiar with it, a product of the industrial revolution.'[32] Similarly, the enthusiasm and skill displayed by medievalists in describing merchants, bankers, textile

30. On the concept of 'tertiary sector' see Clark, 1957; Bauer and Yamey, 1951, pp. 741–55; Minkes, 1955, pp. 366–73.
31. Fourastié, 1949, p. 74.   32. Frankfort, 1951, p. 57.

manufacturers, and town-life mostly had the effect of concealing from the average cultivated person – and often from the medievalists themselves – that even the most highly developed European societies of the Middle Ages remained fundamentally agrarian. The fraction of the active population and resources engaged in trade and manufacture was small, most of the trade itself was connected with agricultural products, the famous merchants and bankers were generally part-time landlords (as most of the artisans and sailors were part-time peasants) and finally – as we shall see later – by far the greatest part of the energy used was actually derived from agriculture.

The Agricultural Revolution of the tenth millennium B.C. and the Industrial Revolution of the eighteenth century A.D., on the other hand, created deep breaches in the continuity of the historical process. With each one of these two Revolutions, a 'new story' begins, a new story dramatically and completely alien to the previous one. Continuity is broken between the cave-man and the builders of the pyramids, just as all continuity is broken between the ancient ploughman and the modern operator of a nuclear station.

In this context the term 'Revolution' is certainly not intended to mean that the changes involved represented sudden accidents unrelated to previous situations and evolutions. It is all too clear that the Industrial Revolution was the product of the cultural, social, and economic changes that had occurred in Western Europe between the eleventh and the seventeenth centuries.[33] And though we know almost nothing about the origin of the Agricultural Revolution, we are convinced that the way was paved by changes in 'the level of culture' as well as in the 'natural condition of the environment'.[34] Each 'Revolution' had its roots in the past, but each

33. Cipolla, 1967, pp. 15–36.
34. Braidwood, 1961, p. 100, and 1960, p. 134.

'Revolution' created a deep break with the very same past.[35] The first 'Revolution' transformed hunters and food-gatherers into farmers and shepherds. The second one transformed farmers and shepherds into operators of 'mechanical slaves' fed with inanimate energy.

35. About the 'invention of farming', Professor Clark wrote that 'to treat a process so long-drawn out and involving so subtle a change in the attitude of men to animals and plants in the same terms as an invention or even a series of inventions in the sphere of technology is surely to misunderstand its nature'. He concludes that 'the Neolithic Revolution was neither a revolution nor was it neolithic; it was rather a transformation begun by Advanced Paleolithic and carried through by Mesolithic communities' (Clark, 1969, pp. 71-2). In a similar vein, referring to the Tehuacán sequence in the New World (see above p. 22), Dr MacNeish wrote that 'it took some 6000 years for the Neolithic traits to evolve into a single complex. This would certainly better suggest a Neolithic evolution rather than a Neolithic Revolution' (MacNeish, 1965, p. 93). I do not question the wisdom of the remarks by Clark and MacNeish. All definitions are *ad hoc* and their validity rests on what one wants to demonstrate. In this book I am using the term Neolithic or Agricultural Revolution not in relation to speed but in relation to the revolutionary character of a change that, no matter how rapid or how slow, transformed hunters and gatherers into shepherds and farmers.

CHAPTER 2

The Sources of Energy

MAN has 'wants' which he likes to regard as 'needs'. He has basic physiological needs for food and drink. He has other elementary wants for clothing and heating. Finally he has, as it were, 'high standard' wants, like reading, listening to music, travelling, amusing himself. Human wants have no upper limit, but they have a lower limit – the minimum food necessary to maintain life.

The nature, magnitude, and form of human wants vary with cultural and geophysical environments, with class, with age, body size, sex, type, and degree of activity. The range of differentiation is indeed wide for the less elementary wants. But even for the very elementary ones there are noticeable differences.[1]

Man satisfies his various wants in vastly different ways,

1. Of two populations with the same age structure and average body size, one living at a mean annual temperature of 25° C. will need about seven per cent fewer calories than an equivalent population living at a mean temperature of 10° C. The influence of body size is such that, other things being equal, a population in which the average male adult weighs 65 kilograms will need about fifteen per cent more calories than a population in which the average man weighs only 50 kilograms. At the same body weight, adult females require about twenty per cent fewer calories than adult males of the same age. It is also estimated that among adults of the same size, the caloric need declines at the rate of about five per cent for each decade after the age of thirty (Keys, 1958, pp. 28–9). If we define arbitrarily a reference man as a man of twenty-five years of age, weighing 65 kilograms, healthy and fit for active work, living in a temperate zone (mean annual temperature 10° C.) and working eight hours a day in an occupation which is not sedentary but does not involve more than occasional periods of hard physical labour, then we may assume that such a man requires on an average, for the entire year, 3200 kcal/day. The work of a coal-miner has never been found to involve an expenditure of more than 4000 kcal/day. This figure can be

using an extremely varied 'basket' of commodities and services – bread, meat, wine, milk, cotton, wool, fuel, paper, steel, electricity, gas, and so on. One way of keeping an account in real terms of such an extraordinarily heterogeneous 'basket' is to refer to the energy value of each item. The unit of account generally used is the 'calorie'. A 'kilocalorie' (kcal) represents the equivalent of the amount of heat required to raise the temperature of one kilogram of water by one degree centigrade. One kilowatt-hour is equivalent to 860 kilocalories.[2] One horsepower-hour is equivalent to 641·7 kilocalories and one British Thermal Unit to 0·252 kilocalories.

Despite its apparent simplicity, this system of accounting is somewhat problematical and can be dealt with only by allowing a considerable margin of approximation. One of the main difficulties is afforded by the conversion of equivalents: their assessment involves arbitrary calculations in the attempt to express one form of energy in terms of another, to evaluate average efficiencies, load factors of major applications, and the power of machines in service.

'Just as a ball of celluloid poised on a jet of water from a fountain will keep its place and spin so long as energy is there, so life depends upon that flow of energy'.[3] Energy is the capacity to do work and various forms are recognized, but those of greatest importance to living organisms are mechanical, chemical, radiant, and heat energy.

---

taken as the upper limit of food requirement. At the other extreme, sedentary clerks expend about 2400 kcal/day (Passmore, 1962, p. 388).

2. When calculating the number of kilowatt-hours produced in a thermic power station on the basis of the kilocalories of fuel burned, the approximate ratio of 2700 kcals = kWh is generally adopted. This ratio is, however, conventional and arbitrary because the actual ratio varies according to the type of fuel and the type and age of the station.

3. Hartley, 1950, p. 105.

All organisms must work to live and they therefore require potential energy to be utilized. Man needs energy as all other living organisms do. He requires daily some 2000 to 3500 calories depending on sex, age, work, and environmental conditions. In addition he requires daily $4\frac{1}{2}$ pounds of water and 30 pounds of air. On the other hand man produces energy. Most of his energy intake is lost in the form of heat: a grown adult irradiates heat equivalent to that of a 75 watt bulb. Of the remaining energy part is used in chemical processes, part (about 10 per cent) leaves the body as waste product, and some portion finally appears as nervous and mechanical activity. We cannot adequately measure the energy value of the nervous activity, but we can evaluate approximately the energy value of the mechanical activity. It has been calculated that the average efficiency of the human body as a machine varies from 10 to 25 per cent depending on the type of work, the speed with which it is done, and the skill of the individual who is doing it. Mechanical efficiency of muscular work can be markedly affected by training. Improvements as great as 37 per cent are quoted in the scientific literature. But it is generally admitted that for sustained work the maximum human efficiency to be expected is about 18 per cent of the energy input.[4]

Man can use his energy output to master and utilize other forms of energy. The more successfully he does so, the more he acquires control over his environment and achieves goals other than those strictly related to animal existence.[5] 'Man', wrote Carlyle, 'is a tool-using animal. Weak in himself and of small stature, he stands on a basis, at most of the flattest soled, of some half square foot insecurely enough. . . . Three quintals are a crushing load for him; the steer of the field

4. Amar, 1920, pp. 186–98; Pyke, 1950, p. 27.
5. For a broad approach to the subject see Ostwald, 1909; Zimmermann, 1951, Chapter 5; White, 1954.

tosses him aloft like a waste rag. Nevertheless he can use tools. Without tools he is nothing. With tools he is all.'

THE CONVERSION OF ENERGY

Energy is available to man when he comes to know about its sources and is capable of mastering it in an economical way. Then the main problem is how to transform this energy into specific form at a selected time and place and at convenient cost.

To solve this problem man must make use of various types of converters. A steam engine, for instance, is a converter that transforms heat energy into mechanical energy when and where desired. It must be remembered that every transformation of energy involves consumption and losses. The output of useful energy (that is to say, into the final form required) obtained by transformation is always less than the energy input. The technical efficiency of a converter is determined by the arithmetical ratio between useful output and total input. Very often, various successive transformations are necessary to be able to obtain energy in the form and at the moment that it is required. This, naturally, involves successive losses which are determined by the rate of the technical efficiency of the various converters successively used.[6] For example, modern boilers can convert about 88 per cent of the chemical energy in the fuel into heat; modern steam turbines transform heat into mechanical energy with an efficiency of approximately 47 per cent; generators can then convert up to 99 per cent of the mechanical energy produced by steam turbines into electricity. Thus the overall efficiency of the whole system of converters used for the production of electricity from mineral fuel is determined as follows:

6. C.E.C.A., 1957, pp. 14–15.

$$\frac{88}{100} \times \frac{47}{100} \times \frac{99}{100} = 41\%.$$

The *economic* efficiency of a converter is measured by the cost per unit of useful energy that the converter produces as compared with the cost per unit of useful energy produced by alternative converters. The cost of useful energy produced by a converter is determined by a set of variables such as the technical efficiency of the converter, its cost of production, its durability and obsolescence, the cost of operating it, and the prevailing price of the source of energy it uses.

From our point of view, plants and animals can be justifiably considered as converters. The sun is the primary source of energy. It releases energy by the nuclear transmutation of hydrogen to helium, and it is on this energy that life on earth depends. The quantity of solar energy entering the earth's atmosphere is approximately $15 \cdot 3 \times 10^8$ cal/m^2/yr. Solar radiation at the ground (direct sunlight plus skylight) varies from a maximum of 200 to 220 kilocalories per square centimetre per year in a desert area to a minimum of 70 kilocalories per square centimetre per year in polar regions. Tropical rain forests receive from 120 to 160 kilocalories; much of Europe 80 to 120. Only green plants can utilize this energy to build up complex organic compounds. However, of the total amount of sunlight reaching the ground only about 25 per cent is of wavelengths that stimulate photosynthesis. Through the process of photosynthesis, plants transform solar light, water, carbon dioxide, and minerals into organic materials containing in various proportions the three main components of human food, i.e. carbohydrates, proteins, and fats. In short, plants are converters that transform sunlight into a form of chemical energy.

Edible animals are converters in so far as they transform one form of chemical energy into another that man finds

39

more suitable or valuable. In fact, edible animals can assimilate plants or parts of plants that man cannot himself digest, and transform them into animal proteins and fats that man can assimilate. Furthermore, since animal proteins are of greater nutritive value than carbohydrates, man occasionally finds it convenient to use animals as converters even when he feeds them with plants that he could use directly.

From a purely technical point of view, most plants and animals are not very efficient converters. The efficiency with which various plant species convert the radiant energy of the sun into the chemical energy of plant protoplasm is referred to as photosynthetic efficiency. In natural populations of plants, photosynthetic efficiency is usually of the order of 1 to 5 per cent. Animals in building up their body tissues, which may serve as food for man, dissipate a large proportion of the chemical energy of plant protoplasm as heat. Growth efficiencies of beef cattle raised on grassland are of the order of 11 per cent net and 4 per cent gross.[7]

By eating plants man gets only a fraction (1 to 5 per cent) of the solar energy that reached the plants. By eating animals man gets only a fraction of the chemical energy contained in the plants the animals had eaten, i.e. a fraction of a fraction of the energy input of the plants. Thus, from the point of view of the quantity of ultimate useful energy produced, the combined plant-animal converter suffers from a double loss. It has been calculated that, compared to corn production, beef production has only about ten per cent efficiency in land utilization for calories of energy: in other words, imagine a small area of land which produces 30,000 calories a day in the form of corn. This amount of food would support about ten

7. Gross growth efficiency is the ratio of calories of growth over calories consumed while net growth efficiency is the ratio of calories of growth over calories assimilated. For all these problems see Phillipson, 1969.

people. If, however, the corn is used to produce beef, the 30,000 calories of corn would yield approximately 3000 calories in the form of meat and 3000 calories will support only one person instead of ten. This is the fundamental reason why poor societies rely more on vegetable carbohydrates than on animal proteins. Actually a plant may be eaten by an animal which in its turn is eaten by another and this second one may itself be eaten by a third animal and so on. Such a sequence of events is termed a food-chain. At an average ecological efficiency of 10 per cent, for every 1000 calories of plant material consumed by herbivores only 100 calories are passed on to carnivores, and of these a mere 10 calories reach the next level of carnivores. These simple facts explain why:

(a) the number of links in any food chain rarely exceeds five;

(b) for man to make the maximum use for food of the solar energy trapped by plants, he should become herbivorous;

(c) in the event of man remaining an omnivore, the most economic use of solar energy when converted to the chemical energy of animal protein is the consumption of herbivore flesh. The majority of man's domestic food animals are in fact herbivorous.[8]

Man, however, makes use of animals not only as food. Domesticated animals provide man with mechanical energy. The efficiency of draught animals in their role of converters that transform chemical energy (fodder) into mechanical energy can be estimated by the range of three to five per cent.[9]

When *homo sapiens* appeared on the earth, he found plant and animal converters already in existence. For many thousands of years – in fact for the greater part of his history – *homo sapiens* remained incapable of doing anything better

8. For all that precedes see Phillipson, 1969.
9. Baum, 1955, pp. 289–91; Pirie, 1962, p. 408.

than moving around trying to capture or to collect any edible plant or animal in sight. His knowledge was basically limited to what was edible and what was not.

Such a state of affairs cannot have been very comfortable. Man spent all his time and energy in the search for food, relying mainly on good luck and his ability to kill wild animals or other men. Starvation was a constant threat, forcing people to infanticide and cannibalism. Furthermore, since man had not yet learned to domesticate animals[10] and knew no other source of energy, his muscles were the only mechanical power he could command.

In a number of myths, animals are credited with having possessed fire before man. Fantastic as they seem, these myths probably contain a grain of truth. Modern archaeologists do not exclude the possibility that the sub-human Australopithecus mastered fire, though the matter is still open to discussion. Undoubted evidence of the use of fire comes from the cave of Choukoutien (China), where fossil remains of a group of Sinanthropi have been found. This would prove that fire was mastered in Asia at some time between 450,000 and 350,000 B.C. In Europe the technique probably arrived later. The first sure indications came from English and Spanish archaeological sites dated around 250,000–200,000 B.C.[11]

Though fire was discovered very early, not all Paleolithic human groups came to know or take advantage of it. Some hunters used fire and some did not. It is also established that those who made use of fire in the most distant past used it only

10. The dog was already domesticated in Mesolithic times, at least by the eighth millennium B.C., but as Piggot (1965, pp. 33–4) points out, 'domestication in this instance does not involve any change in the basic economy, it merely intensifies and renders more efficient the techniques of hunting, like inventing a new type of trap or an improved fish-hook', Cf. also Zeuner, 1963.

11. Oakley, 1955, pp. 36–48; Oakley, 1956, pp. 102–7. On the Australopithecus in particular see also Dart, 1959, pp. 156–8.

for warmth or for protection from predatory animals. Cooking was a development of the late Pleistocene.

Fire allowed man to convert inedible plants to his use, thereby increasing the energy at his disposal. Use of this energy for warmth also allowed him to adventure into hitherto inhospitable areas.

In time, *homo sapiens* made progress in another direction. As indicated in the previous chapter, man perfected his hunting and killing techniques and developed special skills in working stone, preparing primitive tools and taming the dog.[12] In all these discoveries, however, including the use of fire, man merely increased his efficiency in exploiting the two groups of biological converters, plants and animals. Fundamentally he remained a parasite, though an increasingly efficient one.[13] In this situation, the 'economy' could expand without prejudice to its future prosperity only up to the point at which the annual destruction of animals and plants equalled the rate at which animals and plants were replacing themselves. Any expansion beyond this crucial point could take place only at the cost of contraction in the future. To break this bottleneck man had to learn how to control and increase the supply of plants and animals or to discover new sources of energy. These two problems were to be solved by the Agricultural and the Industrial Revolutions respectively.

12. For a first approach to the subject see Boraz, 1959, pp. 36–52, and the important bibliography that he quotes on pages 104–6. On the significance of the domestication of the dog, see above, p. 42, n. 10.

13. How efficient the 'parasite' could be is indicated by the size of animal ossuaries left by Paleolithic hunters. More than ten thousand horse skeletons have been counted at Solutré (France), and nearly a thousand mammoth skeletons have been found at Predmost (Czechoslovakia).

THE AGRICULTURAL REVOLUTION

Indeed, the Agricultural Revolution consisted in the very process whereby man came to control, increase, and improve the supply of disposable plants and animals.

As indicated in Chapter 1, we do not know why or how this Revolution came about. We know that it developed after the end of the last glaciation. It is highly probable that climatic changes played their part. It is also reasonable to suppose that the people who first started to domesticate plants and animals had developed powers of observation and experimentation. In all likelihood cultural developments of some relevance preceded the Agricultural Revolution.

We are on firmer grounds when we try to assess the main consequences of the Revolution. Developing control of the supply of the two groups of biological converters – plants and animals – meant first of all the possibility of a much larger and more dependable supply of food. The first animals to be tamed, beside the dog, were the sheep and the goat. Dairy farming was practised in Mesopotamia at least as early as 3000 B.C. Domestication not for flesh, milk and hides alone but for transport was a relatively later development. The recognition of castration as a means of subduing the uncomfortably potent bull occurred in Western Asia before 4500 B.C. The taming of the steppe horse did not occur before the first half of the second millennium B.C. (Lower Volga and Hungarian region). The taming of the forest horse took place by the beginning of the second millennium B.C. in Sweden and could have taken place elsewhere.[14] Majumdar places the appearance of the horse in India at c. 2500 B.C.[15] The domestication of the bull and of the horse gave man a completely new supply of mechanical energy. In the domestication

14. Zeuner, 1963, pp. 201–44 and 299–337; Piggott, 1965, pp. 35–6 and 95–7.   15. Majumdar, 1965, vol. 1, p. 198.

of plants, a main reason for the importance of cereal grains was precisely that they were capable of being stored for long periods without serious deterioration.

The total amount of energy that the human species could dispose of – chemical energy from edible plants and animals, heat from plants, power from draught animals – increased at a rate inconceivable in the old Paleolithic societies.[16] Populations expanded in size beyond any former 'ceiling'. Villages sprang up and community life emerged. Accumulation of a social surplus became possible. Social groups emerged which became free of the continuous search for food. With the division of labour higher forms of activity and leisurely speculation became possible. New and vast historical possibilities opened up. To use a term generally adopted by archaeologists and anthropologists, the stage of 'savagery' was over.

The ten millennia or so that separate the beginning of the Agricultural Revolution from the beginning of the Industrial Revolution witnessed a great number of discoveries and innovations that increased man's control over energy sources.

There were endless improvements in agriculture. New kinds of plants were domesticated. Plants already domesticated were diffused and acclimatized to various climates and soils.

16. At this point one should emphasize the peculiar and individual quality of the Old World developments as compared with developments in prehistoric America. In America mixed farming, involving the domestication of the larger mammals as well as the growing of a cereal crop, was never achieved until the modern period of European contact. The absence of suitable wild species, and therefore the failure to achieve by domestication an efficient draught animal as an alternative to human traction and labour meant that the civilization that could be built in the Americas was necessarily founded on a wasteful expenditure of human labour for which no alternative nor amelioration could be devised, cf. Clark and Piggott, 1965, pp. 172–3. In the *Account* of his voyages made to New England in 1638 and 1663, John Josselyn acidly remarked (p. 99), 'Tame cattle they (the natives) have none, except lice and doggs'.

And in this very process, all were improved. A good example is offered by maize, which in six thousand years or less evolved from a small wild grass bearing tiny ears no larger than a modern strawberry into one of the world's most productive cereals.[17]

At the same time, special tools and techniques were invented. Sometime between 6000 and 3000 B.C. the plough and the hoe-stick were developed.[18] The prehistoric and ancient oriental ploughshares were made of wood and could not be worked in other than so-called 'light soils'. But soon the technique of working metals was discovered. By 3000 B.C. iron ores were occasionally smelted in Mesopotamia. Iron objects dated 3000 B.C. have been found in Sumerian Ur and in Middle Egypt. After 1400 B.C. iron was smelted and worked on a large scale. The adoption and the diffusion of the iron ploughshares and other new metallic agricultural tools opened 'heavy soils' to cultivation. The Greek and Italic civilizations would not have been possible without these developments.

Discoveries and advances were also made in irrigation, artificial fertilization, and land rotation. Three-field crop rotation was probably already known in classical Greece as early as the fourth century B.C.[19] All these developments were refined through the centuries, in classical and medieval times, by different societies according to the particular needs and requirements of the various environments. It was a slow but irresistible accumulation of knowledge, enriched day by day by experience and practical observation and transmitted from generation to generation, from region to region.

17. Mangelsdorf, 1954, p. 410.
18. On the history of the digging stick, the hoe, the plough, and various agricultural techniques see, among others, Forde, 1955, pp. 378–93 and 432–7.
19. Heichelheim, 1956, p. 326.

Parallel developments occurred in man's exploitation of the 'non-sapientes' living creatures. More animals were domesticated,[20] improved by hybridization, and diffused over larger geographical areas. Important progress was also accomplished in putting to use the mechanical energy of draught animals. The discovery of the wheel, the technique of harnessing, and the invention of the horseshoe were events of paramount importance.

We do not know exactly when the wheel was discovered. But we do know that wheeled vehicles were used in Sumeria and in the Indus Valley about 3000 B.C. Their use spread into Egypt, and possibly China, before 1500 B.C. The earliest example of a wooden cart-wheel in Europe is from a Neolithic trackway in the Netherlands which has been dated provisionally as 1900 B.C. Until recent times, however, wheeled vehicles were not used extensively for inland transportation because of lack of suitable roads and bridges.[21]

Man learned very early how to harness horses and oxen to carts and ploughs. This was a great step in making use of the mechanical energy of draught animals and the technique of harnessing was gradually improved in the course of time. The ox was more easily harnessed than the horse. Since the neck of the ox projects forward from the body horizontally, unlike the rising crest of the horse, and since its vertebral column forms a bony contour in front of which a yoke can easily be placed, a satisfactory harness was easily devised in the earliest times. But this solution was quite inapplicable to the horse. The oldest type of equine harness, the throat-and-girth

20. On the history of animal domestication see Zeuner, 1963.

21. Needham, 1954, vol. 4, part 2, pp. 73 ff. The forward steering was not discovered until the fourteenth century of our era (Gille, 1956, p. 79), and in any case carts could not be extensively used for transportation before a network of satisfactory roads had appeared. Until very recently the pack-mule, the elephant, and the camel carried most of the goods overland.

harness, consists of a girth surrounding the belly and the posterior part of the costal region, at the top of which the point of traction is located. In order to prevent the girth being carried backwards, the ancients combined it with a throat-strap which crossed the withers diagonally and surrounded the throat of the animal. The inevitable result of this was to suffocate the horse as soon as it attempted to put forth a full tractive effort, thus reducing the efficiency of the animal. Despite its inadequacy, the throat-and-girth harness enjoyed an immense spread both in space and time. We find it in Chaldean representations from the beginning of the third millennium B.C. onward, in Sumeria, Assyria and Egypt from 1500 B.C. Western Europe and Islam knew nothing else until A.D. 600 and it was still in use in parts of the Old World in the last centuries of the Middle Ages. In the course of time, however, more efficient types of equine harness were developed. In China the first breast-strap form of harness appeared sometime around the third century B.C. In China again, the perfectly efficient collar harness appeared in the first century B.C. It spread to Europe around the ninth century A.D.[22]

Another important contribution was the discovery of the horseshoe. Archaeological excavations in Austria suggest that it was invented by the Celtic inhabitants of the Alps about 400 B.C.,[23] but it became widely adopted in Western Europe only very much later. Without it a horse or ox working on hard ground wore out its feet rapidly, and a minor foot injury might permanently disable an otherwise useful and healthy animal. The introduction of the horseshoe made both horse and oxen much more efficient and durable.

Mention should also be made here of tools such as the hammer, the tongs, the saw, the potter's wheel, the loom, the press, the various types of gears, the lever, the screw, the

22. Needham, 1954, vol. 4, part 2, pp. 304–30.
23. Heichelheim, 1956, p. 325.

wedge, and the pulley (which, incidentally, does not seem to have been known to the builders of the pyramids). The oldest surviving example of the potter's wheel is from Ur, dated 3250 B.C. It was regularly used in Crete by the beginning of Middle Minoan times, and spread over the Mediterranean by Greek, Etruscan and Punic colonizers. There is no evidence of spinning and weaving before Neolithic times, although the early hunting peoples used cords and threads for fastening, binding, and sewing. Vegetable fibres and wool were among the earliest materials spun and woven throughout the Middle East and Egypt. Fragments of linen dating from about 4500 B.C. were found at Fayum. The oldest cotton fabric is from Mohenjodaro, India, and is dated about 2500 B.C. The discovery of such techniques and their improvements remain unfortunately anonymous and belong to the most shadowy chapter of history.[24]

All that has been said illustrates the fundamental character of the developments that occurred between the Agricultural and the Industrial Revolutions. Such developments were increasing the efficiency of man's use of his own muscular energy, and of the plant and animal converters. Indeed it seems as if the human species spent centuries and millennia in improving the basic Neolithic discovery. The most important exceptions to this general trend were the watermill, the windmill, and the sailing boat.

The story of the invention of the water-mill is complicated. As Professor Needham writes, 'perhaps the horizontal water-wheel and the vertical water-wheel were two entirely distinct inventions'. On the other hand the comparative dating of water power as between China and the West clearly constitutes a puzzling case of approximate simultaneity. Water-

24. Derry and Williams, 1960, pp. 244–60; Needham, 1954, vol. 4, part 2; Cole, 1965.

mills were known in the West in the first century B.C. but for at least two centuries their number remained small.[25] According to some authors it was only when slave labour grew scarce that the water-mill was adopted throughout Western Europe.[26] The explanation may be too simplistic but it is a fact that the breakthrough occurred in the Middle Ages. In medieval Europe water-mills were no longer used only for grinding grain and pressing olives but were applied to other productive activities such as the production of cloth, beer, paper, and iron, as well as 'to turn various machines to make copper pots and weapons of war, to pound herbs, to spin silk, polish arms and saw planks'.[27] The use of water-mills in cloth production accounted for an extraordinary growth in textile manufacturing in thirteenth-century England.[28] By the end of the eighteenth century in Europe there were more than half a million water-mills, and a large number of them had more than one wheel. In China the appearance of the water-mill was more or less contemporary to its appearance in the West. Paradoxically enough, however, the first mention of water-mills in China is not in connection with the turning of millstones but with the complicated job of blowing metallurgical bellows.[29]

Windmills appeared in Persia in the seventh century A.D. The Persian windmill had a vertical axle. The Northern Chinese must have been acquainted with the Persian windmill during the thirteenth century. In Europe windmills appeared towards the end of the twelfth century. A persistent tradition has maintained that the idea of windmills was brought back by the first crusaders. The Western windmill, with the axle

25. Moritz, 1958, pp. 134–9; Derry and Williams, 1960, pp. 250–2.
26. Bloch, 1935, pp. 538–63; Gille, 1956, pp. 67–9.
27. Gille, 1954; Bautier, 1960.
28. Carus-Wilson, 1941, pp. 39–50.
29. Needham, 1954, vol. 4, part 2, pp. 366–435.

horizontal, was, however, from the beginning so different from the Persian as to make it almost a new invention.[30] It spread rapidly from Normandy to France, England, the Low Countries, Northern Germany and the Baltic area, while in Central and Eastern Europe it appeared only after the fifteenth century.

Sailing boats appeared very early, and were soon adopted over much of the world. The first known indication of their existence is preserved in the British Museum. On two predynastic vases of Amratian style from Middle Egypt we find depicted something that is undoubtedly a sailing boat. The date of the vases is probably about 3500 B.C. There is also plenty of evidence to indicate that sailing boats were plying the Eastern Mediterranean by 3000 B.C.[31]

The discovery and diffusion of these three converters – the water-mill, the windmill, and the sailing boat – allowed man to harness the energy in water and wind. The boat especially proved capable of great contributions to economic growth. It was not pure accident that all the great civilizations of the past developed around navigable rivers or on the shores of small, internal, easily navigable seas.

Nevertheless, the importance of the three new converters must not be exaggerated. Until the Middle Ages man failed to make extensive use of water-mills and windmills, and even when they became more generally favoured, their technical characteristics severely restricted their adoption to certain geographical areas and to particular sectors of economic activity. Furthermore, both water-mills and windmills had a limited power per unit. By the thirteenth century, the water-mills in the West had wheels of 1 to 3·5 metres diameter with

30. Usher, 1959, pp. 172–3; Needham, 1954, vol. 4, part 2, pp. 555–68; Derry and Williams, 1960, p. 254.
31. Le Baron Bowen, 1960, pp. 117–31. The two vases are catalogued as numbers 36326 and 35324.

a corresponding power of 1 to 3·5 h.p. By the seventeenth century, it was possible to make wheels of ten metres diameter, but the majority of the mills were still built with wheels of 2 to 4 metres diameter. Builders preferred to increase the number of the wheels rather than to deal with all the problems involved in the concentration of energy on one single wheel. Windmills had more power, reaching easily the average range of 10 to 30 h.p. per unit, but for obvious reasons the windmills never became as widespread and common as the water-mills. The boat had a much wider range of possibilities. But until the thirteenth century A.D., navigation, partly for technical reasons and partly because of defensive needs, continued to rely heavily on manpower, while using the sail only as a complementary source of energy.[32]

One should probably note in passing that, since very ancient times, coal, asphalt, oil, and natural gas had occasionally been used as fuel for heating and lighting in specific areas. However, these were definitely isolated and exceptional cases and their relevance in the overall supply of energy remained quite negligible.

In conclusion, it is safe to say that until the Industrial Revolution man continued to rely mainly on plants, animals, and other men for energy – plants for food and fuel, animals for food and mechanical energy, other men for mechanical energy. The use of other available sources – mainly wind and water power – remained limited. There is no evidence for precise quantitative assessments, but on the basis of general

32. One may recall the Phoenician and Roman galleys, the Viking boat, the medieval Mediterranean galley, and the Polynesian sailing canoe. It is also worth noticing that sails took very long to reach the northern countries. They allegedly appeared in Holland in the first century A.D. and as late as 560 A.D. the Byzantine historian Procopius wrote of the English, 'Those barbarians do not use the sail but depend wholly on oars'. The use of the sails spread to the Viking countries during the sixth and eighth centuries A.D. (Brøndsted, 1960, p. 18).

traits one may venture to say that eighty to eighty-five per cent of the total energy income at any time before the Industrial Revolution must have been derived from plants, animals, and men.

Obviously the exact proportion in which wind and water supplemented the other basic sources of energy varied from society to society and from time to time. The degree of efficiency with which all available sources were exploited also varied in the same way. Cultural patterns and institutions, levels of technology, conditions of war or peace, and geophysical environment were responsible for these differences. Whatever the reasons, the *per capita* availability of energy must have varied markedly from one agricultural society to another. One needs no particular arguments to be convinced that the average *per capita* consumption of energy in Western Europe must have been much higher during the thirteenth century than during the seventh or that the average Roman of the first century A.D. must have controlled much more energy (without taking slave labour into account) than any early Neolithic cultivator of Jarmo in the fifth millennium B.C.

Yet, the fact that the main sources of energy other than man's muscular work were always plants and animals must have set a limit to the possible expansion of the energy supply in any given agricultural society of the past. The limiting factor in this regard is ultimately the supply of land. It should be added that despite more or less continuous progress, the efficiency at which plants and animals were exploited remained relatively low until the Industrial Revolution. At the end of the seventeenth century A.D. the yield ratios for wheat on good soils in the more advanced areas of Europe still stood around 5 and 8 and rarely reached 10.[33]

It is impossible – not to say irrelevant – to calculate what

33. Slicher Van Bath, 1963, pp. 47–53.

could have been the theoretical maximum *per capita* supply of energy in an agricultural society before the Industrial Revolution with an optimum state of technology, optimum distribution of income, optimum cultural and social environment, optimum supply of capital, and so forth. But a very rough estimate of the historical maximum is probably not impossible. In fact, if one considers contemporary agricultural societies – where, to some extent, the use of new sources of energy has been developed – one may venture to say that, apart from a few primitive tribes that carried to an incredible extent the practice of burning wood, most of the agricultural societies of the past must have had an overall *per capita* consumption of energy below 15,000 calories per day – possibly less than 10,000. And most of the actual consumption was put to food and warmth. The diffusion of slavery was just one of the consequences of this general scarcity of other forms of available energy.

THE INDUSTRIAL REVOLUTION

If the Agricultural Revolution is the process whereby man came to control and increase the supply of biological converters (plants and animals), the Industrial Revolution can be regarded as the process whereby the large scale exploitation of new sources of energy by means of inanimate converters was set on foot.[34] Looking at things from this point of view, one easily understands the key role played by the cultural

34. Traditional emphasis on the cotton industry may easily pull out of shape our views of the true nature of the Industrial Revolution. As has been aptly written, the development of English textile manufactures in the late eighteenth and early nineteenth centuries 'fits better as an appendage to the evolution of the old industry than in the way it is usually presented as the beginning of the new . . . There is continuity between the eighteenth century development of Lancashire and the West Riding and the things [of] the pre-industrial revolution world.

revolution of the sixteenth and seventeenth centuries in the shaping of the destiny of mankind.[35] It was, in fact, that cultural revolution that gave to man the conceptual tools which enabled him to master new sources of energy. The conscious systematic investigation of phenomena revealed in man's environment became a fundamental cultural trait of early modern Europe since the days of the Renaissance. In the north-western part of Europe the sixteenth and seventeenth centuries witnessed also a most remarkable mercantile development which favoured the accumulation of physical wealth and of entrepreneurial skills. In England these cultural and economic developments happened to coincide with a shortage of a traditional form of energy (timber) and the presence of large supplies of coal. It was, as W. S. Jevons once wrote, the 'union of certain happy mental qualities with material resources of an altogether peculiar character' that provided the explosive formula.

It all started with steam. 'Steam is an Englishman', as the old saying goes. In the second half of the eighteenth century, James Watt perfected previous discoveries and constructed a steam engine with technical and economic characteristics that led to its wide adoption. He began his experiments around 1765. Commercial use came after 1785 and to a greater extent after 1820.[36] Steam engines were used in metallurgical and textile activities as well as in mining coal and in surface transportation. As more machine power made it possible to produce more coal and to transport it at an

There might have been no Crompton and Arkwright and still there could have been an Industrial Revolution' (Hicks, 1969, p. 147).

35. For an account of the philosophical and scientific developments after 1500 see Stearns, 1943; Hall, 1954; Jones, 1961; Dijksterhuis, 1961; Boas, 1962; Butterfield, 1962.

36. By 1820 in Birmingham there were only sixty engines with a 'total steam-power in horses' of 1000. Cf. Hartley, 1950, pp. 108–9.

enormously accelerated rate, more coal meant in its turn more machine power.

Coal became a strategic element in the emergence and diffusion of the industrial civilization.[37] It meant a rapidly expanding supply of energy that could be used for heating and lighting and for power in sea and land transportation and in almost all the various forms of industry. 'Coal', wrote Jevons, 'stands not beside but entirely above all other commodities. It is the material energy of the country, the universal aid, the factor in everything we do. With coal almost any feat is possible or easy; without it we are thrown back into the laborious poverty of early times.'

Around 1800 the world production of coal amounted to about fifteen million tons per annum. By 1860 it amounted to about 132 million tons per annum with an energy equivalent of about 1057 million megawatt-hours. By 1900, the production had increased to about 701 million tons with an energy equivalent of about 5606 million megawatt-hours. By 1950 the corresponding figures were 1454 million tons and 11,632 million megawatt-hours (Table 4a). The number and capacity of steam engines grew rapidly throughout the nineteenth century (see Table 3).

A cumulative interaction was soon set in motion. The extraordinary growth in the supply of energy stimulated economic growth, which in turn stimulated education and scientific research leading to the discovery of new sources of energy.

Successive improvements were brought to the steam reciprocating engine, and in 1844 the use of steam as a motive power was eventually revolutionized by the invention of the steam turbine. A Parsons turbine was first installed in a power station in 1890 in Newcastle and again in Cambridge in 1892.

37. Wrigley, 1962.

TABLE 3. *Capacity of all steam-engines (in thousands of horse-power)*

	1840	1850	1860	1870	1880	1888	1896
Great Britain	620	1290	2450	4040	7600	9200	13,700
Germany	40	260	850	2480	5120	6200	8080
France	90	270	1120	1850	3070	4520	5920
Austria	20	100	330	800	1560	2150	2520
Belgium	40	70	160	350	610	810	1180
Russia	20	70	200	920	1740	2240	3100
Italy	10	40	50	330	500	830	1520
Spain	10	20	100	210	470	740	1180
Sweden	—	—	20	100	220	300	510
Netherlands	—	10	30	130	250	340	600
Europe	860	2240	5540	11,570	22,000	28,630	40,300
U.S.A.	760	1680	3470	5590	9110	14,400	18,060
World	1650	3990	9380	18,460	34,150	50,150	66,100

In the meantime, in the 1850s, James Young, a Scottish chemist, had established the basis for oil refining. People then became avidly interested in petroleum. Traditionally oil was brought to the surface in buckets by workmen who lowered themselves into hand-dug wells. In 1857, Col. Edwin L. Drake bluntly told the world, 'I can strike oil by drilling through solid rock'. He got in response hoots and jeers but 'Drake's folly' eventually paid off. Having secured the help of a blacksmith and his two sons who were willing to be his 'drillers', on the Saturday afternoon of 27 August 1859 Drake's drill suddenly dropped six inches into a crevice and oil came roaring to the surface. The drill had penetrated 69½ feet (21 metres) of the Pennsylvania earth and rock. The next afternoon Drake started pumping and he filled every empty whiskey barrel in Titusville with the black fluid. By the next year, 1860, over 600 oil companies were incorporated in Pennsylvania. So began the development of the American oil-well industry, marking a turning point in the history of petroleum. In 1860 the French engineer J. E. Lenoir patented a gas engine. About fifteen years later Dr N. A. Otto constructed a gas engine on the principle of the four-stroke cycle. In 1885, Benz's and Daimler's cars, with petrol engines working on the Otto cycle, took successfully to the road.

At the beginning of the nineteenth century, the phenomena of electricity were of purely academic interest. In 1822, however, Michael Faraday caused a wire carrying an electric current to rotate round a magnetic pole. In 1831 he discovered the principle of the transformer and in the same year he also discovered that electricity could be generated by rotating a copper disk between the poles of a magnet. Thus was born the electrical industry. By 1870 practical types of generators were already available to produce either direct or alternating current. In those years Edison invented the incandescent lamp. At the Vienna Exhibition of 1883, practically all the electric appliances of modern life, such as electric hotplates, pans, cushions, and sheets were shown, but the great consumption of electricity followed the evolution of the incandescent lamp. This stimulated the growth of network distribution and the production of huge quantities of electricity in power plants, lowering the cost per kilowatt-hour until other electrical appliances became economical to use.[38] The first great hydro-electric scheme was the gigantic Niagara Falls project which was set to work in 1895 (but so little experience had accrued in the transmission of electric power that at the time the Niagara scheme was launched in 1886 the Company had not even decided what to do with the power harnessed from the waterfalls).

Under the impact of all these discoveries, the process quickened. The more energy was produced, the more energy was sought. Man turned to the sun, the tides, earth-heat, tropical waters, and atmospheric electricity. Then, toward the middle of the twentieth century, he discovered that energy

38. Forbes, 1958, p. 292.

TABLE 4a. *World production of inanimate energy, 1860–1970*

Year	Coal	Lignite	Petrol-eum	Natural gasoline	Natural gas (milliard m^3)	Water power (million megawatt-hours)	Total
		(millions of tons)					
1860	132	6	—	—	—	6	
1870	204	12	1	—	—	8	
1880	314	23	4	—	—	11	
1890	475	39	11	—	3·8	13	
1900	701	72	21	—	7·1	16	
1910	1057	108	45	—	15·3	34	
1920	1193	158	99	1·2	24·0	64	
1930	1217	197	197	6·5	54·2	128	
1940	1363	319	292	6·9	81·8	193	
1950	1454	361	523	13·6	197·0	332	
1960	1809	874	1073		469·0	689	
1970	1808	793	2334		1070·0	1144	
		(million megawatt-hours electricity equivalent)					
1860	1057	15	—	—	—	6	1078
1870	1628	30	8	—	—	8	1674
1880	2511	58	43	—	—	11	2623
1890	3797	97	109	—	40	13	4056
1900	5606	179	213	—	75	16	6089
1910	8453	271	467	—	162	34	9387
1920	9540	394	1032	14	254	64	11,298
1930	9735	493	2045	78	575	128	13,054
1940	10,904	798	3037	83	867	193	15,882
1950	11,632	902	5439	163	2088	332	20,556
1960	14,472	2184	11,159		4971	689	33,475
1970	14,464	1982	24,274		11,342	1144	53,206

Source: O.N.U., 1956, pp. 27–8. The figures for 1960 and 1970 were kindly calculated for me by Professor Paretti.

could be obtained from atoms through the process of fusion or fission.

All these developments have brought about an extraordinary increase in the amount of energy available to man.

Table 4a illustrates this development and its basic components.

The total world production of inanimate commercial energy amounted to about 1·1 milliard megawatt-hours in 1860. By 1900 it had risen to about 6·1 milliard and by 1960 it had reached about 33 milliard. The curve indicates an overall average rate of growth of about $3\frac{1}{4}$ per cent compounded annually. There are reasons to believe that the productive curve overstates the growth of energy requirements during the period 1860–1900 when there was a considerable displacement of fuel wood, etc., by commercial sources of energy. On the other hand it understates the rise in requirements during the period 1900–1950 because these years brought great increases in the efficiency of energy utilization. Actually, for the half-century 1900–1950 it seems reasonable to believe that the rate of growth of world requirements of useful energy during periods free from war and depression was not less than 4 per cent per year and may have reached 6 per cent per year.[39]

The growth of energy production in the long run was much greater than that of population. Thus the average world *per capita* supply increased throughout the last century. Overall world *per capita* averages, however, mean very little. The increase in the supply of energy was by no means equally proportionate to that in population in the different parts of the world. The net result is a great inequality in world distribution of consumable energy. Table 4b illustrates this fact, showing data on *per capita* consumption of inanimate energy for selected countries. The same table shows that there is definitely a rough correlation between *per capita* income and *per capita* consumption of inanimate energy. It is also evident that industrialized countries tend to have a *per capita* consumption of inanimate energy higher than 20 megawatt-hours (= 20·000 kilowatt-hours) per year. The figure is still

39. O.N.U., 1956, pp. 11–13.

TABLE 4b. Per capita *product (1950) and consumption of energy (1952) in selected countries*

	Per capita product ($)		Energy consumption per capita (megawatt-hours)
	A	B	
U.S.A.	1830	1830	62·1
U.K.	1133	875	36·6
France	968	714	18·8
U.S.S.R.	816	—	13·0
Italy	545	321	5·5
India	—	—	2·7

Per capita products in column A are valued by U.S.A. prices and in column B by European relative prices. Figures on energy consumption include firewood and oil shale consumption.

increasing, while more and more countries are rapidly moving in the same direction. It seems therefore reasonable to say that at an advanced stage of industrialization the *per capita* energy requirements tend to move beyond the level of 50 megawatt-hours per year.

It is rather important to realize that high *per capita* consumption of energy not only means more energy for consumption, heating, lighting, household appliances, cars, etc., but also means more energy for production, i.e., more energy available per worker and therefore higher productivity of labour.

For purely descriptive purposes, it can be useful to make a distinction between animate or physiological energy (generated in plants, animals, bacteria, moulds, fungi, etc., and in its turn divided into biotic and muscular energy) and inanimate or purely physical energy (derived from wind, water, wood, peat, fossil fuels, other minerals, tidal motion, heat of the earth, radioactive elements, etc.).

From this point of view, one can say that the Industrial Revolution, by introducing large-scale exploitation of new sources of energy, dramatically changed the patterns of the energy budget of human societies. At an agricultural level any human society disposes of a very limited *per capita* supply of energy, largely physiological. At an industrial level, the energy supply is much higher and mainly inanimate. In the United States, for instance, the contribution of coal, liquid and gaseous fuels, and water-power to aggregate energy consumption passed from less than 10 per cent of the total in 1850 to more than 95 per cent around 1950.[40]

Available inanimate energy is partly derived from recurrent or inexhaustible sources, such as water-power, wind, and wood. Direct solar energy should also be included in this group (the adjective *direct* is used here because water power, wind, and wood are in essence converted solar energy). Other inanimate energy is instead derived from irreplaceable sources, such as coal, lignite, petroleum, and natural gas.

Hitherto the Industrial Revolution had been based essentially on the exploitation of inanimate energy derived from irreplaceable sources. By 1970, more than two thirds of the world energy income was derived from irreplaceable assets.

The irreplaceable assets are coal, petroleum, natural gas, and lignite. They have been formed from carbon dioxide and water in living organisms by the influence of solar radiation. They are 'stored sunlight'. One can summarize the story of our happy generations in the following way. For millions and millions of years wealth was stored and cumulated. Then, someone in the family discovered the hoard – and started to dissipate it. We are now living through this fabulous dissipation. Humanity is today consuming more coal in a single year than was generated in a hundred centuries or so during the process of carbonization.

40. Schurr and Netschert, 1960, p. 36.

The problem arises: how long can the dissipation last? World population today is increasing faster than ever. Energy requirements are increasing at an even faster rate because of industrialization of underdeveloped societies and the further progress of the developed ones. The question of the 'life expectancy' of fossil fuel reserves is becoming a very pressing one. Many estimates of it have been made in recent years;[41] some are pessimistic, some are optimistic. Everyone admits, however, that the day will certainly come when fossil fuel reserves are exhausted.

In the long view of human history, 'man's reliance on fossil fuels for his supply of energy can be but a short episode'.[42] Figures 6a and 6b vividly illustrate this point. Proper alternative sources of energy that can substitute for fossil fuel must be found to prevent mankind from reverting to an agricultural level of activity which would mean a dramatic and painful reduction of both mankind's size and its levels of living. Current scientific discoveries are offering more than one solution, but practical exploitation of these discoveries will largely depend on the capacity of human societies to build up the capital required for trapping economically the more 'difficult' kinds of energy. Indeed, 'it involves a great deal more work to live on income than on the accumulated capital of geological ages'.[43] The substitution of inexhaustible for irreplaceable sources of inanimate energy is a main problem of the second phase of the Industrial Revolution. But it is not the only one.

Around 1952, the annual world production of energy (including vegetable fuels and animal energy) was in the neighbourhood of 29 thousand million megawatt-hours. Of these, only some 10 thousand million were actually put to work.

41. See Schurr and Netschert, 1960, p. 295, and Hubbert, 1971, pp. 31–40.
42. Thirring, 1958, p. 218.   43. Darwin, 1953, p. 75.

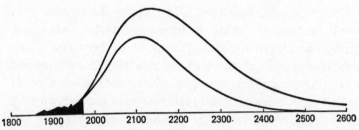

Fig. 6a. World coal production. The top curve reflects an estimate of $7 \cdot 6 \times 10^{12}$ metric tons as the amount of usable coal; the bottom curve reflects an estimate of $4 \cdot 3 \times 10^{12}$ metric tons. The curve that rises to the top of the graph shows the trend if production continued to rise at the present rate of $3 \cdot 56$ per cent per year. The amount of coal mined and burned in the century beginning in 1870 is shown by the black area at the left. (From 'The Energy Resources of the Earth' by M. King Hubbert. Copyright © 1971 by Scientific American, Inc. All rights reserved.)

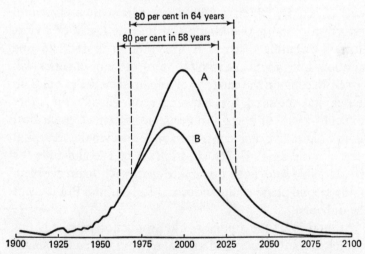

Fig. 6b. World oil production is plotted on the basis of estimates of the amount of oil that will ultimately be produced. Curve A reflects an estimate of 2100×10^9 barrels and curve B represents an estimate of 1350×10^9 barrels. (From 'The Energy Resources of the Earth' by M. King Hubbert. Copyright © 1971 by Scientific American, Inc. All rights reserved.)

64

TABLE 5. *World's energy income, 1952*

PRODUCTION	Milliards megawatt-hours electricity equivalent
coal	12·0
lignite & peat	1·3
petroleum & natural gasoline	7·7
natural gas	2·7
water power	0·4
vegetable fuels	4·6
animal energy	0·3

29·0 of which 10·4 produced in North America

                      5·5 „ „ W. Europe

LOSSES		5·0 „ „ E. Europe &
in processing plants	3·6	U.S.S.R.
in transmission	0·1	
in use	14·0	
other	1·1	

18·8

PRODUCTION LESS LOSSES

10·2 of which 0·3 used in agriculture

               0·8 „ „ transportation

               5·8 „ „ industry

               3·3 „ „ household

Source: O.N.U., 1956, pp. 3–35.

The others – two-thirds of total production – were *lost* (Table 5).

Energy can be lost in all sorts of ways. There are production and transportation losses. There are losses in the process of the interconversion of fuels. And finally there are heavy losses in the conversion of heat to mechanical energy, such as the generation of unwanted heat, the evaporation of cooling water, mechanical friction, improper combustion, imperfect heat transfer, and a low load factor. The largest losses occur at the consumer level, where nearly half the original supply of energy is today dissipated in the form of waste heat in the course of its use.

All this means that man is still extremely inefficient in the use of inanimate energy. In a way, we are like the first neolithic farmers. They were definitely inefficient in the use of the converters – plants and animals – that they had just learned to control. It took man thousands of years and an endless chain of discoveries to improve his efficiency in exploiting the basic discovery of the Agricultural Revolution. Similarly, a great deal of progress is still needed to reach a satisfactory degree of efficiency in the utilization of inanimate converters. The long march has already begun. The steam engine of Watt had a technical efficiency of 5 per cent while modern steam

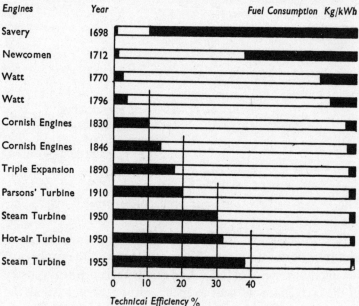

Fig. 7a. The technical efficiency of steam engines, 1698–1955
(from Thirring, 1958)

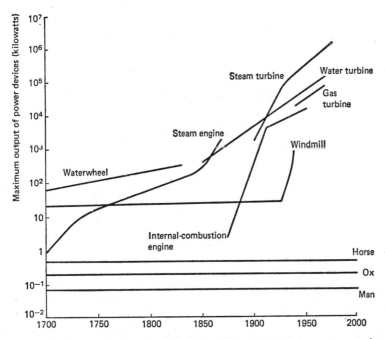

Fig. 7b. Improvements in technical efficiency of various types of machines. (From 'Energy and Power' by Chauncey Starr. Copyright © 1971 by Scientific American, Inc. All rights reserved.)

turbines reach 40 per cent (Figs. 7a and 7b). The most dramatic increase in fuel-conversion efficiency in this century has been achieved by the electric-power industry. In 1900 less than 5 per cent of the energy in the fuel was converted to electricity. Today the average efficiency is around 40 per cent. The increase has been achieved largely by increasing the temperature of the steam entering the turbines that turn the electric generators and by building larger generating units. These are quite remarkable improvements, but there is still a long way to go.

The problem with inefficiency is that the costs resulting from it do not consist solely in waste but also in actual damage. The wasted residuals from improper treatment of

67

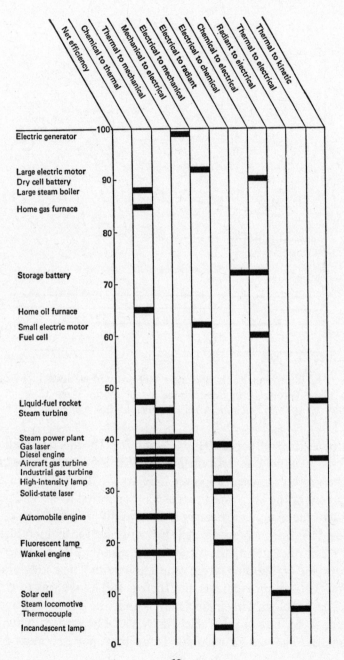

fuels are rapidly poisoning the environment, disturbing delicate ecological equilibria – they may even be damaging our genetic inheritance.

In 1965 in the U.S. the energy conversion sector as a whole obtained four per cent output from hydroelectric generators, 0·1 per cent from nuclear fuel, and the remainder was derived from fossil fuels. Given our present inefficiency, we have to regard fossil fuels as 'dirty'. While putting to use their energy content, we discharge into the environment huge quantities of carbon monoxide, hydrocarbons, sulphur dioxide, oxides of nitrogen, particulates, wasted heat and noise.

What we must avoid is finding ourselves with the mines exhausted and the pollutable reservoirs filled up.

Fig. 7c. Efficiency of energy converters runs from less than 5 per cent for the ordinary incandescent lamp to 99 per cent for large electric generators. The efficiencies shown are approximately the best values attainable with present technology. (From 'The Conversion of Energy' by Claude M. Summers. Copyright © 1971 by Scientific American, Inc. All rights reserved.)

CHAPTER 3

Production and Consumption

MAN needs capital to trap energy. And still more capital to exploit obtained energy for productive purposes. Capital accumulation is a necessary condition for any society's survival and progress. And, conversely, any society's survival and progress is in a way a measure of that society's capacity to accumulate capital and use it efficiently.

There is definitely a correlation between capital and output. In a hunting economy, the capital needs are very limited: a few bones – used as tools or as weapons – and (in more developed cultures) bows, arrows, and stone implements. In an agricultural economy the capital needed is of quite a different quality and magnitude: stocks of seeds, fertilizers, ploughs and other implements, draught animals, silos, mills, boats, wagons, and so forth. In an industrial economy, capital needs are still more complex and much larger: machinery, railways, chemical and atomic plants, dams, research laboratories, and so forth. The greater the production, the greater the volume of capital needed. On the other hand, it is also true that the greater the production, the greater the possibility of capital formation.

We do not possess enough information about the patterns of production, consumption, and capital formation in a hunting economy. In this chapter we will limit our analysis to the patterns generally prevailing in agricultural and industrial societies.

THE AGRICULTURAL SOCIETY

Capital is made possible by saving. If resources are consumed they are obviously not available for capital cumulation. If you eat your cow today you cannot hope to have your milk

70

tomorrow. Only by forgoing present consumption can a society cumulate capital. It is generally admitted that in any agricultural society, given the low *per capita* income, *per capita* saving is – in absolute terms – rather low. This circumstance is badly aggravated by the way saved resources are used. Temples, pyramids, mansions, jewellery, warfare, and so forth generally absorb a large quota of resources squeezed out of current income. Furthermore, pre-industrial societies are typically characterized by inadequate transport facilities. Mass transportation is generally non-existent and communications are costly and insecure. Consequently any pre-industrial society must keep inventories in much larger proportion to current production than any industrial society does. This is true for any type of commodity, but particularly so for basic necessities. Such inventories are a form of investment, i.e., of capital accumulation, but with a 'stabilizing' character. Generally investment of a 'developmental' character is very small in any agricultural society.

It has been indicated that a society needs different amounts of capital at different stages. In order to pass from, let us say, an agricultural type of economic organization to an industrial one, a society must make substantial efforts to build up the capital necessary for the transition. If this transition is gradual, the process can be relatively smooth. If, on the contrary, the transition is forced to take place in a very short time, the process is bound to be painful. In such a case, 'industrial' capital must be squeezed out from an income that is still 'agricultural'. The more abrupt the transition, the greater the hardships.

To accomplish the transition, a given society must reach an absolute level of capital formation, a sort of 'critical minimum level', failing which the transition is not possible. But an agricultural society cannot industrialize by increasing beyond the 'critical minimum' the total volume of wooden ploughs or hoe-sticks produced, any more than hunters can become farmers by increasing their output of flaked stones and arrows. Indeed, the required changes in capital formation are of a qualitative as well as of a quantitative nature. The qualitative changes imply that the active population must acquire new skills, and that the total population must adopt new patterns of living. This problem will be discussed later in Chapter 6. Here we only have to remember that the need for new skills may mean that further capital is needed for investment in education.

In all agricultural societies of our past we find that, mainly because of limitations of energy sources known and exploited, the great mass of people could hardly afford to satisfy anything but the more elementary needs, food, clothing, and housing, and even these at rather unsatisfactory levels. Correspondingly, most of the available resources are employed in agriculture, textile manufacture, and building.

Of these three sectors, agriculture is always by far the predominant one. It absorbs the greatest quota of available capital and labour. Further, it somehow represents the pivotal point around which all other activities tend to revolve. Building makes a large use of timber. And textile manufacture uses materials – wool or linen, cotton or silk – that are also produced 'in the fields'.

On the fringe, there is always some trade – in one form or another – heavily concentrated on agricultural products (grains, wines, spices, timber, etc.) and textiles. In terms of labour employed, trade is generally a minor sector, and merchants a minority. But trade always plays a strategically dynamic role. It allows specialization and better use of available resources. Its fluctuations are of paramount importance to the fortunes of the whole economy. All historical records seem to demonstrate that where trade flourished, demographic and economic levels were the highest attainable within the range of agricultural possibilities. Actually, almost all the great agricultural civilizations of the pre-industrial past were founded on the expansion of the mercantile sector. And it was an exaggerated expansion of this sector in seventeenth- and eighteenth-century England that created the preconditions for the emergence of the Industrial Revolution.

THE INDUSTRIAL SOCIETY

Thanks to the exploitation of new sources of energy, larger amounts of capital, and more efficient use of factors of production, *per capita* real income is vastly greater in any industrial society than in any agricultural society. Consequently, the quality of the diet of the mass of people is generally better. Improvements are also generally experienced in clothing and housing. New and 'higher' human wants are satisfied on a mass scale. Actually, expenditure on such 'higher' items as transportation, medical care, education, amusements, etc., increases more than proportionately. Thus, expenditure on food – although increasing in absolute terms – decreases as a percentage of total private expenditure.

In connection with the exploitation of new kinds of energy and new prevailing consumption patterns, one observes a general decline in the relative importance of agriculture, which also suffers from the fact that the other productive sectors tend to lose their dependence on it. The building industry substitutes steel and cement for timber. The textile industry substitutes artificial fibres (rayon, dacron, etc.) for natural ones. The pharmaceutical industry substitutes chemical products for spices and herbs. Even the food industry follows the trend: vitamin pills replace natural fruits, and Coca Cola replaces wine. It has been said that before the Industrial Revolution, of all the things man used, nearly eighty per cent were derived from the plant and animal kingdom, with only about twenty per cent from the mineral kingdom.[1] These figures cannot be accepted at their face value. But they can undoubtedly be taken as orders of magnitude. With the Industrial Revolution the situation they describe is substantially reversed. Correspondingly, both the percentage of total active population employed in agriculture and the proportion of income produced by the agricultural sector shrink markedly while a great expansion is generally experienced in the new key sectors: the chemical, the metallurgical, and the mechanical.

In an industrial society the contribution of science and scientific methods to production is obviously great. Consequently the rate of growth of an industrial society is largely influenced by the amount of resources devoted to research and education and by the efficiency at which these resources are used. This does not detract from the importance of investment in reproducible physical capital, because for much of the new knowledge that becomes available, its incorporation into the productive process requires replacement of existing capital goods by new ones. On the other hand, because of the highly dynamic character of an industrial society, both its physical and its human capital are under the threat of accelerated obsolescence. Vast resources must therefore be devoted to the training and retraining of people just as vast resources are needed for the building and replacement of capital goods.

Statistical material available on the economic development of Europe and the United States during the last hundred years vividly illustrates some of the patterns sketched briefly in the previous paragraphs.

Labour increased because of population growth and in the course of time a progressively larger proportion of it was

1. Mather, 1944, pp. 55–6.

absorbed by the secondary and tertiary sectors at the expense of agriculture. Data on this trend have already been presented in Chapter 1 (Tables 1 and 2), pp. 30 and 31. The absolute volume of capital formation also increased remarkably in the long run. Proportionately it took more and more the form of machinery and producer durable equipment at the expense of construction and inventories (cf. the figures for the United States in Table 6).

TABLE 6. *Net capital formation in the United States (percentage of average values)*

	1869/98	1909/38
Producer durable equipment	14	22
Construction	71	49
Net addition to inventories	18	12
Net charges in claims against foreign countries	–3	17
	100	100

Source: Kuznets, 1946, p. 55.

No less important than the growth of inputs was seemingly the improvement in the efficiency of their utilization. According to some economists, between 1909 and 1949, employed capital per man-hour in the private, non-farm sector of the U.S. economy rose by 31·5 per cent. This increase in capital should have given rise to an increase in *per capita* output of about 10 per cent. Output per man-hour rose instead by 105 per cent. Calculations of this kind are not as precise as they look. They are based on a number of arbitrary assumptions and it is not difficult to show that some of these assumptions are bound to underestimate the contribution of capital equipment.[2] But if specific figures can be questioned, one cannot doubt that in an industrial society a good deal of economic growth is due to technological change, better education of the labour force and non-constant returns to scale.

2. See, for all, Bowen, 1963, and the bibliography quoted.

The growth of inputs (labour and capital) and their progressively more efficient utilization brought forward an extraordinary expansion of production. Production increased faster than population, and thus *per capita* income grew over the long run.

Table 7 summarizes growth of population, national product, and national product *per capita* during the last century in selected countries. Table 8 shows how the importance of the agricultural sector in the formation of aggregate income diminished everywhere. Of course all figures are tentative and are subject to large margins of error.

The key role in all this development was played by the industrial sector.

Between 1901 and 1955 the volume of 'industrial production'[3] increased in the United States at an average of 3·7 per cent per year, industrial product per head at an average of 2·4 per cent per year. In Western Europe,[4] the volume of 'industrial production'[5] increased at an average of 2·3 per cent per year, and industrial product per head at an average of 1·6 per cent per year.

All these figures are tentative and subject to large margins of error. Specifically the figures of Tables 7, 9 and 10 must be taken with one important reservation. Given our crude way of measuring industrial production and national income, the statistics for produced wealth include both by-products which are undesirable and goods and services needed to get rid of the unwanted by-products. However, even when all this is taken into consideration, one cannot deny that the production

3. 'Industrial production' is here defined as production resulting from mining, quarrying, and manufacturing.

4. For the definition of Western Europe as referred to in this chapter see Table 10.

5. 'Industrial production' is here defined as for the United States (see footnote 3, p. 76) with the addition of the production of electricity and gas.

TABLE 7. *Rates of growth of population, national product, and product* per capita *at constant prices in selected countries from the mid-nineteenth to mid-twentieth century*

	Initial period	Terminal period	Per cent average change per year		
			Population	National product	National product *per capita*
United Kingdom	1860–69	1949–53	0·8	2·2	1·3
France	1841–50	1949–53	0·1	1·5	1·4
Germany	1860–69	1950–54	1·0	2·7	1·5
Sweden	1861–8	1950–54	0·7	3·6	2·8
Italy	1862–8	1950–54	0·7	1·8	1·0
Russia & U.S.S.R.	1870	1954	1·3	3·1	1·5
United States	1869–78	1950–54	1·7	4·1	2·0
Canada	1870–79	1950–54	1·8	4·1	1·9
Japan	1878–87	1950–54	1·3	4·2	2·6
Australia	1898– 1903	1950–54	1·7	2·8	1·0

Source: Kuznets, 1959, pp. 20–21.

TABLE 8. *Percentage share of agriculture in national income of selected countries*

	1770	1870	1970
Canada			5
France		45	6
Germany		30	3
Great Britain	45	15	3
Italy		57	9
Japan		63	7
Sweden		43	4
United States		30	3
Russia		55	22
India			45
Brazil			14

77

TABLE 9. *World production: energy, pig-iron, steel*

	Energy (milliards megawatts)	Pig-iron (million tons) ·	Steel
1850	—	5	—
1870	1·7	13	1
1900	6·1	40	29
1910	9·4	70	60
1920	11·3	60	72
1929	13·1	100	121
1940	15·9	102	142
1950	20·6	134	189
1960	33·5	260	380

Source: for energy see above, Table 4a, p. 59; for pig-iron, British Iron and Steel Federation, Statistical Yearbook for 1954; for steel, C.E.C.A. 1957 (2), pp. 22–3.

TABLE 10. *Growth of industrial production in Western Europe and United States, 1901–55*

	Population (millions)		General index industrial production (volume) 1938 = 100		Index industrial production per head (W.E. 1955 = 100)	
	W.E.	U.S.	W.E.	U.S.	W.E.	U.S.
1901	195·0	77·6	44	35	37	74
1913	216·6	97·2	69	66	51	109
1929	234·0	121·8	86	124	60	165
1937	245·7	129·0	102	127	67	160
1955	284·1	165·2	177	291	100	285
1960	300·3	180·7	231	334	124	298

W.E. = Western Europe = O.E.E.C. Member Countries (Austria, Belgium, Denmark, France, Germany, Greece, Ireland, Italy, Luxemburg, Netherlands, Norway, Saar, Sweden, Turkey, United Kingdom).

Source: Paretti and Bloch, 1956, Table 2, 28, and 30. Data for 1960 were kindly calculated for me by Professor Paretti.

of wanted goods and services increased dramatically in the West over the period 1800 to 1970 as did the standard of living. The overall growth of the world production vastly increased the degree of interdependence of the various countries. As a matter of fact, a very rapid expansion of long distance communications and international trade was at the same time both a condition and a result of the economic development of the world.

TABLE 11. *World's railways mileage and shipping*

	Railways (thousand miles)	Merchant vessels sailing ships	steam ships
		(thousand gross tons)	
1850	24	9100	280
1860	67	13,000	780
1870	130	13,500	2050
1880	230	13,870	4400
1890	380	10,540	8285
1900	490	7245	22,370
1910	640	4625	37,290
1930	775	1585	68,025
1950	770	720	84,580

Figures reproduced in Table 11, no matter how impressive, noticeably underestimate the progress of communications. On the one hand they do not take into account the drastic improvements in the velocity of trains and ships and in the control systems of railways which allowed a much more efficient use of the existing capital.[6] On the other hand, the figures of Table 11 must be supplemented with figures relating to the progress of motorization, inland water transport and air transport. Between 1948 and 1970 the world's civil air traffic progressed as follows:

6. Rail freight traffic grew from 3,300,000 million net tons-kilometres in 1960 to 5,015,000 million in 1970.

| | *Thousand millions of* | | |
	passenger-kms	Tons - kms freight	mail
1948	21	0·4	0·2
1958	85	1·7	0·5
1970	385	10·7	2·8

The growth of industrial production both in Europe and the United States was accompanied by a marked shift in the relative importance of the various sectors of industrial manufacture. We have already referred to this phenomenon and its causes in the previous paragraphs. Let us assess some of its quantitative aspects. At the beginning of the twentieth century, food and textiles together covered 47 per cent of total manufacturing production in Western Europe and 44 per cent in the United States. By 1955 the two sectors represented only 21 per cent in Western Europe and 19 per cent in the United States.

During the same period the share of metal products increased from 16 to 34 per cent in Western Europe and from 10 to 41 per cent in the United States. Chemicals similarly passed from 5 to 14 per cent in Western Europe and from 5 to 13 per cent in the United States. Altogether by 1955 the metal products and chemicals sectors accounted for 48 per cent of total manufacturing production in Western Europe and 54 per cent in the United States.[7]

The expansion of *per capita* real income allowed drastic improvements in the levels of living and the satisfaction on a mass scale of other than elementary wants. The following indicators may be used to demonstrate the levels of consumption that any industrial society reaches – or exceeds:

7. Parallel changes occurred in the commodity composition of international trade, cf. Baldwin, 1959, p. 55, table 5.

PRODUCTION AND CONSUMPTION

Energy consumed *per capita* per year (megawatt-hours)	over	20
Per cent illiterate (population age ten and over)	below	5
Elementary school teachers per 1000 population	over	5
Doctors per 1000 population	over	1
Expectation of life at birth (years)	over	60
All foods: calories *per capita* per day	over	2500
Animal proteins: oz. *per capita* per day	over	1·5
Expenditure on food and drink as percentage of total private expenditure	below	40
Percentage of population in the age group 18 to 25 attending school	over	25

Indicators such as '*per capita* consumption of energy' or '*per capita* GNP' or 'annual freight carried *per capita*' or 'number of telephones and cars per 10,000 people' are very popular among economists, but they can be extremely deceptive. While they are a crude measure of levels of consumption, they are often taken as a measure of human welfare – which is wrong. Consumption and welfare are two totally different things. As K. E. Boulding put it, 'The throughputs of a system are essentially costs of the system, not rewards or returns. A country under a pleasant climate, with a population adequately nourished and in good health and a culture that promotes cheap, simple and helpful pleasures may have a much lower *per capita* GNP than a country with a bad climate, a big defence industry, and a culture which promotes individual misery. Yet the people of the former society may be much better off than the people of the latter'.[8]

Once all this has been said one must add that the conditions under which pre-industrial societies lived and live do not even distantly approach the state of being 'adequately nourished, in good health, and with a culture that promotes helpful pleasures'. For the masses of the agricultural societies, the prevailing levels of living have always been those of abject

8. Boulding, 1970, pp. 44–6.

TABLE 12. *Composition of industrial production in Western Europe and United States by major sectors, 1901–55*

	Western Europe					United States				
	1901	1913	1929	1937	1955	1899	1914	1929	1937	1955
Total manufacturing	100	100	100	100	100	100	100	100	100	100
Food	27	19	16	15	13	24	20	14	15	11
Textiles	20	18	14	12	8	20	19	11	12	8
Basic metals	7	10	10	10	9	9	10	10	9	9
Metal products	16	24	27	28	34	10	13	33	31	41
Chemicals	5	6	10	10	14	5	6	8	10	13
Others	25	24	23	25	22	32	32	24	23	18

Source: Paretti and Bloch, 1956, Table 18. For the definition of 'Western Europe' as referred to in this table see Table 10.

TABLE 13. *Per cent composition of private consumption in selected countries, 1950*

	U.S.	U.K.	France	Germany	Italy
Food	22·1	31·3	38·4	41·2	46·4
Alcoholic beverages	1·4	2·0	9·4	2·9	7·2
Tobacco	1·5	1·7	1·2	1·5	1·5
Clothing and household textiles	13·7	12·7	11·3	13·1	15·1
Housing	3·7	5·9	4·6	5·4	4·3
Fuel, light, and water	6·4	7·6	3·0	2·8	1·9
Household goods	15·4	10·0	7·8	9·1	1·4
Household and personal services	2·6	4·4	2·8	2·8	3·5
Transport equipment and services	15·2	5·0	4·8	4·0	4·0
Communication services	1·1	0·7	0·4	0·2	0·3
Recreation and entertainment	5·4	9·4	8·0	8·2	7·4
Health	3·4	4·2	4·7	5·5	1·6
Education	2·6	3·3	3·1	3·1	4·5
Miscellaneous	5·5	1·8	0·6	0·2	1·1
	100·0	100·0	100·0	100·0	100·0

Source: Gilbert, 1958, p. 60

misery. Some industrial societies may feel that they have high consumption but no welfare. Agricultural societies have neither. Today three-quarters of mankind are still tied to agricultural levels of living. They desperately want to be 'adequately nourished and in good health'. Undergoing the Industrial Revolution is their great hope, but perhaps the biggest among the many difficulties that these agricultural masses have to overcome is the fact that they are multiplying themselves at an appalling rate. It is at this point that we have to turn our attention to the population problem.

CHAPTER 4

Births and Deaths

PRIMITIVE hunters and food-gatherers – whether pre-historic men, modern Australian aborigines, or contemporary Eskimos – are always scant in numbers and extremely scattered. Anthropological and archaeological research confirms this proposition. The general consensus is that density among hunting and food-gathering peoples is far too great if it is as much as one person per square kilometre.[1] The population density of contemporary Pygmies in Central Africa is of the order of 0.2 inhabitants per square kilometre. Their biomass is only about twice as high as that of chimps living in a comparable area (3.6 kg/km^2 in the Ghana forest). Probably only a few fishing groups very favourably situated have experienced densities greater than one person per square kilometre. In fact, actual densities varied extremely, not only with area but also with climatic change, the diffusion or disappearance of game, and the growth and decline of various cultures. The density values that one can find for various societies are so vastly different that any average would be meaningless. But the highest densities are so low that they are more significant than any possible average. As Acsádi and Nemeskéri put it, 'judging from the burial places, the size of

1. See Ratzel, 1891, Part II, pp. 255–64; Forde, 1955, p. 376; Krzywicki, 1934, pp. 52–8; Braidwood and Reed, 1957, pp. 21–3; Piggott, 1965, pp. 28 and 32, 'guesses on analogy' averages ranging from three to thirteen persons per 100 square miles. He supposes that 'hunting bands would more likely number twenty or twenty-five people than larger totals; fifty would be the limit . . . in a group of four to five family groups, totalling not more than twenty-five persons, about five would be adult men who could effectively hunt big game'.

Paleolithic populations was probably not larger than one joint family'.

Some time ago the belief was common that early man's fecundity was lower than that of civilized man, and that this was the main cause for the small size of Paleolithic societies. Today this theory is generally disregarded. We do not possess reliable figures, but indirect evidence supports the view that the Paleolithic populations had very high mortality. Since the species survived, we must admit that primitive man also had a very high fertility.[2]

High mortality and high fertility were associated with a short average length of life. Here again we run into the difficulty of extremely poor information and we can express our concept only in rough quantitative terms.[3] By analysing fossil remains of 187 Europeans of the Neanderthal group, Vallois was able to ascertain that 'more than a third died before reaching the age of 20, and the great majority of the rest died between the age of 20, and the age of 40. Beyond this limit, there are only 16 individuals, most of whom certainly died between the age of 40 and the age of 50.'[4] Weidenreich, analysing the fossil remains of 38 individuals of the Asiatic Sinanthropus population (a much earlier group than the Neanderthal) substantially confirmed the results of Vallois. Out of the 38 Sinanthropi it was possible to assess probable age at death for 22. Of these, it seems that 15 died when less than 14 years old, 3 died between the age of 15 and 29, 3 between 40 and 50, and only one seems to have survived beyond 50.[5] These figures are vitiated by a number of factors and their real meaning is highly dubious. They refer to quite

2. Wolfe, 1933, pp. 35–60.
3. On the weaknesses of vital statistics based on human remains cf. Vallois, 1960, pp. 187 and 195.
4. Vallois, 1937, p. 525. Cf. also Vallois, 1960, p. 196.
5. Weidenreich, 1949, pp. 194–5.

different generations of people, they tend to disregard infant mortality and their number is too small to represent a reliable sample. However, evidence collected for hunting-stage societies of historic times generally agrees with these findings. The age of fifty is rarely attained and 'the centre of gravity of these societies moves towards the lower age-groups'.[6]

In regard to causes of death, Weidenreich observed that most of the fossil remains of prehistoric man clearly indicate a violent death.[7] For Paleolithic man of historic time, Krzywicki arrived at a similar conclusion, observing that the most frequent causes of death were infanticide, war, and headhunting.[8] Acsádi and Nemeskéri point out that, in general, death was closely related 'to accidents, violence, and diseases resulting from factors of the natural environment or their changes'.[9] The low density of population was in a way a protection against epidemics. It is indeed difficult to see how, with sparse populations organized into small bands wandering over limited territories, contagious diseases could have had the importance that they have assumed under other demographic conditions. But it is not difficult to believe that starvation and diseases connected with nutritional deficiences must have taken on the whole a heavy toll of human life in Paleolithic and Mesolithic societies,[10] especially among infants.

AGRICULTURAL SOCIETIES

Agricultural societies began very early to be interested in the numbers of their members, either for military or fiscal reasons.

6. Krzywicki, 1934, pp. 243–54. 7. Weidenreich, 1949, p. 196.
8. Krzywicki, 1934, pp. 101–14.
9. Acsádi and Nemeskéri, 1970, p. 181.
10. In regard to illness, all available evidence seems to indicate that primitive man was more resistant to noxious infections by bacteria than modern man. See Weidenreich, 1949, p. 203.

Through interpretation of surviving records and with the assistance of archaeological evidence it is not impossible to reach rough estimates of population totals and densities for ancient societies. On both fertility and mortality, however, there is no information available until a very late period. Records for some areas of Europe start in the late sixteenth century, but this is exceptional. Generally, available records start much later. The careful collection of detailed statistics requires a quantitatively orientated culture and organizational capacities that – apart from a few exceptions – are not characteristic of agricultural or pastoral societies. The evidence that can be derived from funerary inscriptions hardly allows any meaningful conclusion about the average length of life.[11]

However poor, the material available seems to justify some general conclusions. Compared with the data of the Roman era, medieval mortality conditions derived from Central European paleodemographic sources do not reflect substantial changes. Any agricultural society – whether sixteenth-century Italy, seventeenth-century France, or nineteenth-century India – tends to adhere to a definite set of patterns in the structure and movements of birth- and death-rates. Crude birth-rates are very high throughout, ranging between 35 and 55 per thousand and the average number of children born to a 'married' woman (using the term 'married' in its broadest connotation) by the end of her fertile period (at the age of forty-five or fifty) is at least five. Within the above indicated range, the actual value of the birth-rate in any given agricultural society varies according to numerous factors: age and sex composition of the population, sanitary and economic conditions, the prevalence of war or of peace, and,

11. On the great difficulties of estimating the average length of life on the basis of funerary inscriptions see Henry, 1957, pp. 149–52, and Henry 1959, pp. 327–9.

last but not least, socio-cultural factors such as the attitude toward marriage,[12] the attitude toward birth-control etc. Death-rates are also very high, but *normally* lower than the birth-rates – ranging generally between 30 and 40 per thousand.

The population of an agricultural society is characterized by a normal rate of growth of 0·5 to 1·0 per cent per year. To give a meaning to this figure I can quote an exercise in astronomical arithmetic by P. C. Putnam: if the race had sprung from a couple living not long before agriculture was discovered – let us say 10,000 B.C. – and if its members had

12. The percentage of women who get married in the age group 15 to 50 and the age at which they get married strongly influence the number of births in any given society. On the other hand, the attitude towards marriage is strongly influenced by customs and social values. Agricultural societies showed a great variety of attitudes toward marriage. According to the English traveller F. Moryson, at the end of the sixteenth century 'in Italy marryage is indeed a yoke, and that not easy one but so grievous as brethren no where better agreeing yet contend among themselves to be free from marryage and he that of free will or by persuasion will take a wife to continue their posterity, shall be sure to have his wife and her honour as much respected by the rest, besyde their liberall contribution to mantayne her, so as themselves may be free to take the pleasure of women at large. By which liberty they live more happily than other nations. For in those frugall commonwealths the unmarried live at a small rate of expenses, and they make small conscience of fornication, esteemed a small sinne and easily remitted by Confessors' (Hughes, 1903, pp. 156 and 409; Cipolla, 1965, pp. 578–9). In China, on the contrary, Father Matthew Ricci noticed at the end of the sixteenth century that 'celibacy is not approved of and poligamy is permitted' (Gallagher, 1953, p. 97), and at the end of the eighteenth century Barrow (1805, pp. 398–9) noticed that 'public opinion considers celibacy as disgraceful, and a sort of infamy is attached to a man who continues unmarried beyond a certain time of life'. In India pre-puberty marriage became customary after the sixth century A.D. (Kapadia, 1958, pp. 138–66), while in sixteenth-century Germany 'women are seldome marryed till they be twenty fyve yeares old' (Hughes, 1903, p. 296). See also Hajnal, 1965.

expanded at the rate of one per cent per year since then, the world population would form today a sphere of living flesh many thousand light years in diameter, and expanding with a radial velocity that, neglecting relativity, would be many times faster than light.[13] This has not happened because throughout the demographic history of agricultural societies death-rates show a remarkable tendency to recurrent, sudden dramatic peaks that reach levels as high as 150 or 300 or even 500 per thousand. On a few occasions these peaks coincided with wars. But much more frequently they were the result of epidemics and famines that wiped out a good part of the existing population. Reference is often made to the famous Black Death as if it were an exceptional disaster. Admittedly this unfortunate case deserves some special mention, for all Europe was then struck more or less at the same time. But one has to remember that the sudden disappearance of a fifth of the population or a third or even half, was, every once in a while, a recurrent catastrophe of local experience. The statistics collected by Father Mols for medieval and Renaissance Europe offer eloquent evidence of these disasters.[14] The intensity and frequency of the peaks controlled the size of agricultural societies.

A highly fluctuating death-rate is an index of inadequate control over environment. The demographic density of agricultural societies tended to grow out of proportion to their technical capacity to control crop fluctuations and epidemic disease. Whenever a given agricultural population grew beyond a given 'ceiling' the probability increased of sudden catastrophes that would drastically reduce the population itself (see Fig. 10b).

In normal times, a large proportion of the deaths were represented by infant mortality. Of 1000 newborn children,

13. Putnam, 1950, p. 18.
14. Mols, 1955, Vol. 2, pp. 425–84.

200 to 400 usually died within a year. Many of the remaining ones died before reaching the age of seven. A famous sixteenth-century physician, Jerome Cardano of Pavia, used to maintain that he could cure anyone on condition that the patient was not younger than seven or older than seventy.[15]

The high toll of infants and youths drastically reduced the average length of life. All available information for numerous societies seems to indicate that the 'agricultural' life expectancy at birth generally averages twenty to thirty-five years[16] and of those who reach the age of five few have good chances of surviving beyond fifty.[17]

The prevailing high birth-rates have distinctive effects on the age composition of agricultural populations: the number of young people is very high. In general, between one third and one half of the population is below 15 years of age; in other words, the population pyramid of an agricultural society is very broad at its base. From an economist's point of view, this means that the young non-productive population represents a heavy burden for the active adult population and this is one of the reasons why agricultural societies put children to work at an early age.

THE INDUSTRIAL REVOLUTION

The Industrial Revolution changes the general picture drastically again.

15. Cardan, 1962, p. 180.

16. Dublin, Lotka, and Spiegelman, 1949, pp. 28–43; Stolnitz, 1954–5, pp. 27–8; Burn, 1953, pp. 1–31; Bellido, 1955, pp. 117–23; Russell, 1958, pp. 22–32.

17. In comparing these figures with those quoted for the hunting stage, one should remember that remains preserved from Paleolithic times are mostly those of adult people. An average age at death calculated on the basis of the data collected by Vallois or Weidenreich would therefore tend to ignore mortality among infants and children.

Hitherto, all societies that have been industrialized seem to have experienced an almost total disappearance of the recurrent peaks of the death-rate. The reasons are manifold. New scientific knowledge about plants and livestock, extraordinary improvement in transportation, progress in medicine and sanitation – all have allowed men to cope with famines and epidemic diseases. Two of the three main causes of the peaks have been brought under control at least temporarily. Unfortunately, one cannot say the same of the third cause – aggression. Actually the technical progress which enabled man to control famines and epidemics increased his destructive efficiency, and this is one of the elements that cast a sinister shadow on the future of industrial societies.

The Industrial Revolution also made gains possible in regard to what can be called 'normal death',[18] i.e. the death-rate in normal times. Progress in medicine and sanitation, better nutrition, and higher levels of living have practically eliminated many diseases and reduced the incidence of many others. The 'normal' death-rate has been pushed down, and in industrial societies the crude death-rate tends to be below 15 per thousand (Table 14a).

The most important component in the fall of the 'normal' death-rate was a drastic reduction in infant and adolescent mortality. In industrial societies, infant deaths tend to be fewer than 35 per thousand live births (Table 15). The drastic reduction of infant and adolescent mortality contributed noticeably to raise the average length of life. In industrial societies life expectation at birth tends to be over 60.[19]

We shall discuss later the behaviour of the birth-rate under the impact of the Industrial Revolution. Let us just note here

18. Sauvy, 1958, pp. 31–70.
19. Stolnitz, 1954–5; Chasteland, 1960, pp. 58–88. See also Tables 14c and 16.

TABLE 14a. *Crude birth- and death-rates (per thousand) in selected countries, 1750–1950*

	Birth-rates					Death-rates				
	1751 1755	1801 1805	1851 1855	1905 1909	1950	1751 1755	1801 1805	1851 1855	1905 1909	1950
AFRICA										
Egypt				45·2	44·4				26·5	19·1
Union of South Africa (White pop.)					25·1					8·7
AMERICA										
Canada					27·1					9·0
Mexico				46·0	45·5				32·9	16·2
United States				30·0	23·5				15·4	9·6
Argentina				40·0	25·5				20·1	9·0
Brazil					43·0					19·0
Chile			46·6	44·6	34·0			35·0	33·2	15·0
Venezuela				43·6	42·6				29·8	10·9
ASIA										
China					45·0					25·0
India				48·0	24·9				43·0	16·1
Pakistan					19·0					12·2
Japan				31·9	28·2				20·9	10·9

EUROPE										
Austria					15·6					12·4
Belgium				25·1	16·9				16·2	12·5
Denmark				28·4	18·6				14·1	9·2
England & Wales	35·0	34·0	33·9	26·7	15·9	30·0	23·0	22·7	15·1	11·6
United Kingdom					16·3					11·7
Finland	45·3	38·4	36·3	31·0	24·5	28·6	24·7	28·2	17·7	10·1
France	35·0	31·7	26·1	20·1	20·6		26·3	24·1	19·5	12·7
Germany			34·6	32·3	16·2			27·2	18·3	10·3
Greece				33·6	20·0				20·3	7·1
Hungary				36·3	21·0				25·7	11·5
Ireland				23·4	21·3				17·2	12·7
Italy				32·6	19·6				21·7	9·8
Netherlands				30·0	22·7				14·7	7·5
Norway	34·4	28·2	32·5	26·7	19·1	25·0	24·1	17·3	14·1	9·1
Portugal				33·5	24·4				21·6	12·2
Spain				33·7	20·2				24·5	10·9
Sweden	37·1	31·4	31·8	25·6	16·4	26·3	24·4	21·7	14·6	10·0
Switzerland			29·0	26·4	18·1			23·6	16·5	10·1
Yugoslavia					30·3					13·0
RUSSIA			48·0	45·8	26·7			40·0	29·5	9·7

TABLE 14b. *Estimates of the crude birth-rate, 1960–65 and 1965–70, and the gross reproduction rate, 1965–70, in major areas and regions of the world*

Areas and regions	Birth-rate		Gross reproduction rate
	1960–65	1965–70	1965–70
WORLD TOTAL	35·1	33·8	2·3
More developed regions	20·5	18·6	1·3
Less developed regions	42·0	40·6	2·7
EAST ASIA	34·0	31·5	2·0
Mainland region	36·1	33·1	2·1
Japan	17·2	18·0	1·0
Other East Asia	38·7	34·7	2·5
SOUTH ASIA	45·1	44·3	3·0
Middle South Asia	45·4	44·4	3·0
South-East Asia	44·6	44·2	3·0
South-West Asia	44·0	43·6	3·1
EUROPE	18·7	18·0	1·3
Western Europe	18·2	17·5	1·3
Southern Europe	20·7	19·4	1·3
Eastern Europe	17·5	17·3	1·2
Northern Europe	17·9	17·6	1·3

SOVIET UNION	22·4	17·9	1·2
AFRICA	46·9	46·8	3·1
Western Africa	49·0	48·8	3·2
Eastern Africa	46·4	46·6	3·1
Middle Africa	45·0	45·3	2·9
Northern Africa	47·5	46·9	3·2
Southern Africa	40·3	40·7	2·7
NORTHERN AMERICA	22·7	19·3	1·4
LATIN AMERICA	39·1	38·4	2·7
Tropical South America	40·7	39·8	2·8
Middle American Mainland	44·6	43·7	5·1
Temperate South America	26·8	26·3	1·8
Caribbean	36·7	35·0	2·4
OCEANIA	27·1	24·5	1·7
Australia and New Zealand	22·6	20·2	1·4
Melanesia	42·4	41·7	2·9
Polynesia and Micronesia	41·5	39·7	2·9

Source: United Nations, 1971

TABLE 14c. *Estimates of the crude death-rate, 1960–65 and 1965–70, and expectation of life at birth, 1965–70, in major areas and regions of the world*

Areas and regions	Death-rate		Expectation of life
	1960–65	1965–70	1965–70
WORLD TOTAL	15·7	14·0	53
More developed regions	9·0	9·1	70
Less developed regions	18·8	16·1	50
EAST ASIA	16·5	14·0	52
Mainland region	18·3	15·3	50
Japan	7·3	7·0	71
Other East Asia	10·4	9·7	60
SOUTH ASIA	20·3	16·8	49
Middle South Asia	20·9	17·2	48
South-East Asia	19·3	16·1	50
South-West Asia	17·4	15·6	51
EUROPE	10·2	10·2	71
Western Europe	11·0	11·0	72
Southern Europe	9·4	9·3	70
Eastern Europe	9·4	9·5	71
Northern Europe	11·2	11·1	72

SOVIET UNION	7·2	7·7	70
AFRICA	22·8	21·3	43
Western Africa	25·2	24·3	39
Eastern Africa	23·6	21·8	42
Middle Africa	26·1	24·3	39
Northern Africa	19·1	16·9	50
Southern Africa	17·9	17·4	48
NORTHERN AMERICA	9·3	9·4	70
LATIN AMERICA	10·9	10·0	60
Tropical South America	11·1	10·0	60
Middle American Mainland	11·2	10·1	60
Temperate South America	9·3	9·1	65
Caribbean	12·0	10·9	58
OCEANIA	10·2	10·0	65
Australia and New Zealand	8·7	8·7	72
Melanesia	18·2	17·6	47
Polynesia and Micronesia	10·5	8·8	61

Source: United Nations, 1971

TABLE 15. *Infant mortality (total infant deaths per thousand live births) in selected countries, c. 1800, c. 1900, 1950, and 1965–6*

	c. 1800	c. 1900	1950	1965–6
Sweden	190	96	22	13
Low Countries		147	26	14
Norway		88	27	17
Denmark		126	32	19
Switzerland		139	32	17
Great Britain		145	33	20
Finland		135	42	18
France	190	149	53	22
Belgium		153	53	24
Ireland		102	47	25
Germany		207	55	24
Austria		221	66	28
Italy		168	68	34
Spain		195	69	35
Western Europe (average)		148	45	
New Zealand		75	23	18
Australia		97	24	18
United States		162	33	23
Canada			41	23
Japan		151	60	19
Russia		260	81	27
Mexico			96	61
India		232	127	
Chile		264	153	107

Source: Data for Europe are derived from Chasteland, 1960, p. 48. For non-European countries data are derived from Febvay and Croze, 1954, p. 390; Chandrasekkar, 1959, pp. 88–9. For Russia, Kantner, 1960, p. 40, and Urlanis, 1963, p. 91. For the U.S.A., U.S. Bureau of Census 1960, p. 28.

that in any industrial society it tends to range below 20 per thousand (Table 14b) and total fertility is one to three children per married woman by the end of her fertile period. With a low birth-rate, in an industrial society, the population pyramid is relatively narrow at the base and relatively large at the middle and upper sections (see Fig. 8). In the 1950s, in France as in Sweden the people of 65 years of age and over

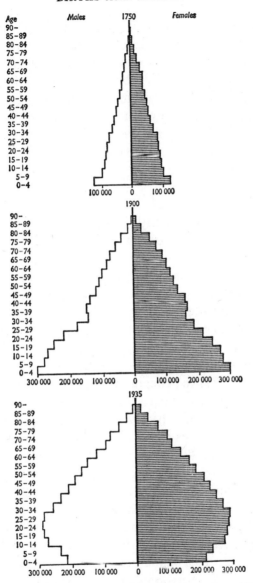

Fig. 8. Population pyramids – Sweden, 1750–1935

Source: Historisk Statistik för Sverige.

were more than ten per cent of the total population. While agricultural societies have to face the problem of how to utilize their large number of children, the industrial societies have to solve the problem of how to utilize their large number of aged people. The problem is not an easy one especially because, given the highly dynamic character of the industrial societies, their old people, instead of being regarded as living repositories of wisdom and knowledge, are considered useless relics of the past.

LEVELLING UP THE BIRTH- AND DEATH-RATES

The preceding observations seem to suggest that for any one of the three basic types of economic organization there exists – at least potentially – an equilibrium mechanism that controls population growth. For the hunting–fishing societies we suppose – rather vaguely, with allowance made for some taboo contraceptive practices and counting infanticide in the death-rate – that the equilibrium mechanism consisted of a high death-rate matching a high birth-rate. How fluctuating these rates could have been we simply do not know. For the agricultural societies we can state more precisely that the mechanism generally consisted of a high and highly fluctuating death-rate that checked a high but more stable birth-rate. The death-rate was normally lower than the birth-rate and the population tended to increase, but eventually catastrophic peaks of the death-rate wiped out the 'surplus' population. Then the cycle started again. For industrial societies it seems that the mechanism should mainly consist in adjustment of the birth-rate to a very low death-rate. The looser the adjustment of the birth-rate to the death-rate, the higher the probability of the reappearance of the peaks as equilibrating devices. 'If we breed like rabbits, in the long run we have to die like rabbits.'[20]

TABLE 16. *Expectation of life at birth and at sixty in selected countries, 1900–50*

	at birth				at sixty		
	W.E.	Russia	U.S.	India	W.E.	Russia	U.S.
ca. 1900	47	32	48	23	14	14	15
ca. 1950	67	67	69	32	17	19	18

W.E. = Western Europe = Austria, Belgium, Denmark, Finland, France, Germany, Great Britain, Ireland, Italy, the Low Countries, Norway, Spain, Sweden, Switzerland. U.S. data refer to white population only. Source: Chasteland, 1960, p. 71, U.S. Bureau of Census, 1960, pp. 24–5, Ts. S. U.S.S.R. 1962, p. 608.

These mechanisms have never been so rigid as to stabilize any population completely.[21] At any stage, the birth- and death-rates have a range of possible variation. Furthermore, and particularly in regard to agricultural societies, periods of peace and prosperity tend to reduce the frequency of catastrophic peaks in the death-rate while periods of war and disorder tend to increase it. These circumstances allow for massive population movements either up or down. The secular demographic 'cycles' of China before the nineteenth

20. Carlson, 1955, pp. 1437–41. There is a long-run incompatibility of noticeably divergent fertility-rates and death-rates. The reason lies in the absurdity of continued geometric increase. See Coale, 1959, p. 36, and also below, p. 118, footnote 7.

21. The term equilibrium has been used in the text above to mean not absolute stability, but rather the lack of any substantial and sustained movement of growth or decline. 'Natural populations tend to fluctuate about some equilibrium figure. This fact has long been recognized by biologists . . . From a short-term point of view, populations are in only approximate equilibriums, but viewed from the time scale of the Pleistocene, slowly expanding populations of man can be considered as being essentially in equilibrium' (Bartholomew and Birdsell, 1953, p. 494).

century[22] and the '*grosse Wellen*' of the German population[23] are typical examples of this kind of movement.

If it is true that the equilibrium mechanisms are flexible enough to allow substantial growth or decline in a population, it is also true that their existence conditions and limits the possible range of movements. Further, movements within the limits allowed by the equilibrating mechanism are generally the product of particular local cultural or political development and are therefore geographically limited.

The 'demographic explosions' that accompanied both the Agricultural and Industrial Revolutions show, on the contrary, very different characteristics. First of all, as they follow the diffusion of the Revolution, they become world wide. Secondly, they tend to be of exceptional intensity and magnitude. It seems really as if, during each Revolution, the population is 'getting out of control'. These explosions may be considered as the result of the disruption of a prevailing equilibrium mechanism. The span of time before a new equilibrium replaces the disrupted one is the period during which the population 'gets out of control'.

We do not have enough information about the first of the two Revolutions to be able to detect how and why one equilibrium was broken and a new one came to replace it. But we are pretty well informed on the explosive mechanism of the second Revolution. Here, the general patterns are as follows. The starting point (equilibrium of the agricultural stage) is a high birth-rate (35–55 per thousand) and a high (normally 30–40 per thousand) and highly fluctuating (up to 150–300–500 per thousand) death-rate. With the Industrial Revolution the ghastly recurrent death-peaks tend to disappear. This fact by itself is bound to start an unusual growth, because the normal death-rate is from the very beginning

22. Ta Chen, 1946, pp. 4–6.
23. Mackenroth, 1953, pp. 112–19.

lower than the prevailing birth-rate and the catastrophic peaks of the death-rate were a vital element in the former equilibrium mechanism.[24] However, this is not the entire story. Under the impact of progress in medicine and sanitation and improvement in the diet of the people, the 'normal' death-rate also undergoes a downward movement. The birth-rate too eventually should follow a downward course but under the pressure of numerous and different cultural, institutional, and economic forces, the birth-rate shows a certain degree of resistance. It adjusts to the pull of the death-rate with a time lag Fig. 9a. The extent of this time lag may be negligible or considerable.[25] France and England (with Wales) offer good examples of different forms of development. In both cases the disappearance of the death-peaks, leaving an uncontrolled gap between the birth- and death-rates, produced a demographic explosion. However, while in France the birth-rate quickly followed the death-rate, in

24. Helleiner, 1957. A good illustration is offered by contemporary India. Between 1891 and 1921 a high and nearly constant level of fertility was combined with relatively high and fluctuating death-rates. Death-rates fluctuated in response to famines induced by crop failures and to the incidence of major epidemics. The result was a very slight rise in population. Over the interval 1891 to 1921 the total growth was little more than 5 per cent, or an average of less than one-sixth of one per cent per annum. After 1921, while the level of fertility and that of 'normal' death remained constant, the sudden and violent peaks of the death-rate due to epidemics and famines disappeared. The absence of major calamities of this sort since 1921 produced a growth rate that over the period 1921–51 has exceeded one per cent per annum: Coale and Hoover, 1958, pp. 29, 31, and 54. The growth of Italian population in the eighteenth and early nineteenth centuries was a similar case, see Cipolla, 1965.

25. In some cases the lag can be further aggravated by the fact that at the very beginning of the process the birth-rate not only does not respond to the 'pull' of the death-rate, but actually tends to move – though only for a short time – in the opposite direction. This can be due for instance to a lowering of the average age of marriage.

103

England and Wales the birth-rate responded to the pull with a noticeable lag and up to 1820 the gap increased considerably, adding new fuel to the explosive growth.

We have been dealing so far[26] with societies that have undergone industrialization. Yet, today, we witness a new interesting development. Industrialized societies, having acquired the technical capacity to control disease, felt and still feel a humanitarian urge to give medical assistance to societies that basically are still agricultural. The consequences of such action are appalling. 'In Europe knowledge of death control was slowly developed and growth of population was therefore gradual. In the underdeveloped countries the accumulated knowledge of two countries is immediately available and death-rates have therefore fallen much faster than they ever did in Western Europe. In Ceylon, to quote an extreme but illuminating case, the malarial mosquito has been wiped out by DDT and deaths fell from 22 to 12 per thousand in the seven years from 1945 to 1952 (immediately after spraying with DDT the death-rate fell from 20 to 14 per thousand in a single year 1946–7), a fall which took seventy years in England and Wales. In Mauritius a fall from 27 to 15 deaths per thousand, which took 100 years to achieve in England and Wales, also came about in seven years.'[27] The suddenness of the fall of the death-rate, combined with the fact that some of the 'underdeveloped' countries are not prepared for the cultural changes that the Industrial Revolution implies (especially in regard to birth-control), causes a dramatic

26. The explanation offered above in the text is generally indicated as the 'demographic transition theory'. While nobody denies the validity of it as a broad description of facts, the theory has been occasionally criticized as representing a more or less unweighted and non-specific collection of associations between broad social and economic trends and fertility. Cf. Van Nort and Karon, 1955.

27. P.E.P., 1956, p. 12. On the case of Mauritius cf. also Holmberg, 1965, pp. 3–29.

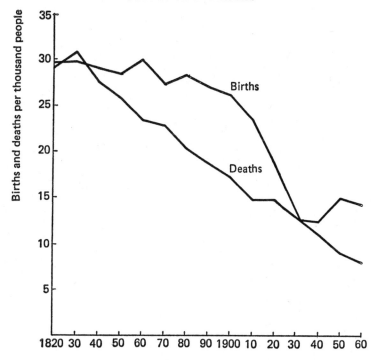

Fig. 9a. The demographic transition in Sweden shown with standardized
rates

widening of the 'demographic gap' (see Fig. 9b). Again
to take Ceylon as an example, the precipitous decline
in mortality was not accompanied by any measurable change
in fertility: the crude birth-rate has remained over 40 per
thousand. [28] In other cases, the drop of mortality was actually
accompanied by a most unwelcome increase in fertility. In
Madagascar one-third of the female population was sterilized
by venereal disease. The medical care introduced by the whites
caused, together with improvements in mortality, a growth in

28. Taeuber, 1956, p. 757; Sarkan, 1957.

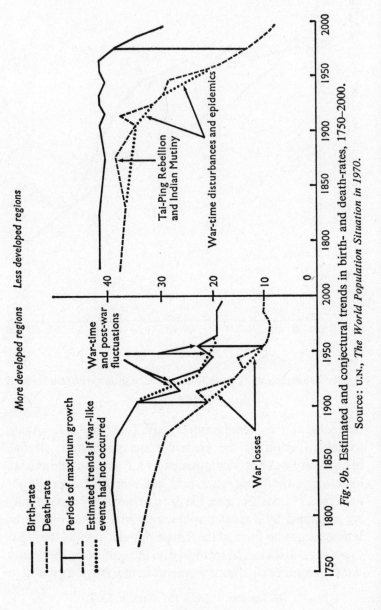

Fig. 9b. Estimated and conjectural trends in birth- and death-rates, 1750–2000.
Source: U.N., *The World Population Situation in 1970.*

106

fertility.[29] With an 'agricultural' birth-rate and an 'industrial' death-rate, the demographic explosion is bound to assume alarming proportions. In Ceylon, the annual rates moved as follows:

	birth-rate (per thousand)	death-rate (per thousand)	rate of natural increase (per thousand)
1900–1909	38	29	9
1910–1919	38	30	8
1920–1929	40	27	13
1930–1939	37	24	13
1940–1949	37	18	19
1950–1959	38	11	27

In Mauritius, the annual rate of natural growth was 5 per thousand in 1936–40 and 29 per thousand in 1958. It was 28·1 per thousand in South-East Asia and 33·6 per thousand in the Middle American mainland in 1965–70 (see Tables 14b and 14c).

From a demographic point of view, all that 'exploding' underdeveloped countries need is to bring down their birth-rates to a manageable level. But the reduction of birth-rates is in some way related to substantial improvements in the levels of living. And these improvements are the more difficult to obtain the greater the population pressure. If the capital output ratio is 3, i.e. 3 units of capital are required to produce 1 unit of income, then, with a population growth of 2 per cent per annum, 6 per cent of the net income has yearly to be invested only to maintain the same level of living for the growing population. With a population growth of 3 per cent per annum, 9 per cent of national income has to be invested to reach the same result. The higher the rate of population growth, the harder becomes the task of breaking through the Malthusian trap. A vicious spiral is therefore set into operation. Because of a high rate of population growth, 'industrial-

29. Olivier, 1935.

ization' is difficult to attain. Because there is no 'industrial-ization' the birth-rate and the rate of population growth remain high. A solution must certainly come. There is a long-run incompatibility between high fertility rates and low death-rates. No matter what technological progress the future brings, in the long run either fertility goes down or mortality goes up. An equilibrium must be reached. But when? And how?

CHAPTER 5

How Many People?

POPULATION GROWTH AND STANDARDS OF LIVING

'My first approach to the population problem was purely mathematical. But it immediately became apparent that in its real essence the problem was a biological one. This conclusion led to its controlled experimental study in the laboratory.' With these words decades ago an American scientist, Pearl, began a book on *The Biology of Population Growth*.

The study he referred to was conducted in a laboratory with a 'suitable creature', *Drosophila melanogaster*. 'It is a small fly, which looks like a diminutive replica of a common house fly, and is seen in swamps around decaying or fermenting fruit, or liquids like cider and vinegar made from fruit and left exposed to the air.' He selected a group – 'Adam and Eve, a few young children (larvae) and a few other children (pupae)' – and enclosed them in a special bottle with appropriate food. Thus he arranged 'a dipteran microcosm, a spatially limited but well-equipped universe'. And he set himself to watch 'nature take her accustomed course'.

'In due time more children will be born, since mère and père are no slackers in the chiefest biological duties and privileges. Some will die. Others will grow up and have offspring of their own. Ultimately the old folks will pass away, but not before there has accumulated around them a great crowd of their descendants of several generations. In short a population will have grown in this little universe.' From censuses of the 'population' at frequent intervals, about every second or third day, the experimenter concluded that 'the fly *Drosophila* in its population growth under controlled experimental conditions follows the logistic curve' (see Fig. 10a).

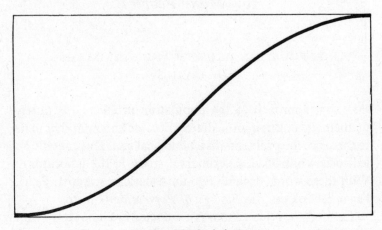

Fig. 10a. The logistic curve

Pearl then spent endless efforts to demonstrate that the growth of human population likewise adheres to the patterns of the logistic curve. And since there are always many people very fond of using simple mathematical tools to explain complex social phenomena, the thesis of the eminent geneticist became quite popular at the time.

Actually, any generalization from Pearl's experiment is rather questionable. The growth of a human population has peculiar elements that differentiate it from the growth of, say, a population of *Drosophila melanogaster*. It is sufficient to remember the unequal distribution of incomes and resources among the human population and the fact that man has learned how to control and to increase, at least within certain limits, the supply of food and resources at his diposal, thereby enlarging through technological and organizational progress the 'bottle' in which he happens to live. Moreover, also among animals, things do not always happen so smoothly as a logistic curve may induce us to believe. Often a population overshoots and in such a case the adjustment to the upper carrying-capacity levels occurs through some minor or major catastrophe (see Fig. 10b). The story of the European population between A.D. 1000 and A.D. 1500 fits better the dramatic model of the curve of Figure 10b than the gentle model of the logistic curve of Figure 10a.

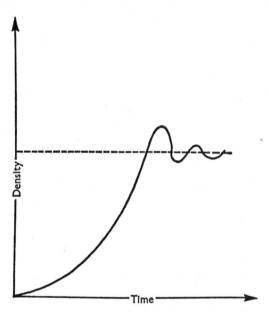

Fig. 10b. A theoretical example of population that has overshot and consequently adjusts through a series of oscillations to the carrying-capacity level

Both models assume that a given population of living creatures tends to expand to the limit of available resources. However, in the social life of many species of superior animals some sort of 'territorial rights' are enforced that prevent the entire species from facing a Malthusian catastrophe. In these cases the burden of Malthusian pressure is made to fall upon a

111

minority of displaced and destitute individuals, and the population is maintained noticeably below the maximum possible density.[1] It can easily be proved that 'territoriality' operates also among men.[2] Furthermore, in the behaviour of human population there are other elements of distinct originality. *Drosophila melanogaster* uses the supply of agar in the bottle just to increase its number. Man uses available resources to increase his numbers, *and* to improve his levels of living. The 'ceiling' to population growth in human societies – at least in non-savage ones – may be set 'not by the carrying capacity at a subsistence level, but by the carrying capacity at a desired or conventional standard of living'.[3]

Which are the mechanisms that allocate resources between the two alternate uses – population growth and better levels of living? The question is open to discussion. Unequal distribution of income undoubtedly played a key role in ancient societies. The emergence of privileged classes of priests and aristocrats has since the earliest days of human history diverted resources to higher modes of living and prevented the increase of available production from being fully absorbed by the growth of population. Uneven distribution of income and the very fact that the rate of growth of industrial

1.'Territoriality' has been discovered by observing the social behaviour of birds and mammals. The effects of 'territoriality' on population have been summarized as follows: 'Should the population increase, local population density does not continue to build up indefinitely. Instead territorial defence forces individuals out into marginal situations, and thus the resources of the optimal habitat are not exhausted. Most of the displaced individuals do not survive, but some may find unexploited areas of suitable habitat and thus extend the range of the species. The result is that population tends to be maintained at or below the optimum density in the preferred habitat, and the excess individuals are forced to marginal areas to which they must adapt or die.' (Bartholomew and Birdsell, 1953, p. 485)

2. Forde, 1953, pp. 373–4; Bates, 1955, pp. 68–76.

3. Taylor, 1955, p. 50.

production remained noticeably above the rate of population growth for a long period must have been key factors during the Industrial Revolution in establishing the higher standards of living that compete with the natural propensity to have children. Imitation of upper classes by lower classes or of 'developed' by 'underdeveloped' societies should also be taken into proper account.

Whatever the reasons and the mechanisms, since its appearance on this planet human society has increased its size and bettered its levels of living. There is of course the question whether the allocation of available resources between 'quantity' and 'quality' has been the best one. We shall discuss this problem later on. Let us for the moment try to assess the quantitative growth.

THE AGRICULTURAL REVOLUTION

It was pointed out in Chapter 1 that all available evidence seems to show that around 10,000 B.C. all – or almost all – the human population on this planet still lived by hunting, fishing, and gathering wild fruits. Chapter 4 then explained that a society of hunters or fishers rarely reached an average density of 1 person per square kilometre. Working on those suppositions, and taking into account the fact that some areas of the Earth are not inhabitable, one can reasonably suppose that on the eve of the Agricultural Revolution there could not have been more than 20 million people on Earth. This figure must be regarded as a maximum. The minimum can be credibly fixed around 2 million. The actual population probably ranged between 5 and 10 million people.[4]

The Agricultural Revolution allowed the species to break this ceiling. Man enlarged Pearl's bottle, and human population increased far beyond any previously possible level.

4. Huxley, 1957, p. 172; Durand, 1958, p. 29; Deevey, 1960, pp. 196-7.

Although the demographic increase can properly be visualized as a consequence of the Agricultural Revolution, one should not overlook the fact that the growth of population may have in its turn fostered the diffusion of the Revolution. The spread of early farming was a process of technological diffusion that can be explained in two different ways, which need not be mutually exclusive. According to the cultural diffusion mode of explanation, domesticated strains and technological know-how would be passed on from one group to another independently of significant geographic displacements of the group. Alternatively the spread can be seen as a function of population growth and displacement. It has been shown mathematically that if population growth coincides with a modest local migratory activity, random in direction, a wave of population expansion will set in and progress at a constant radial rate. Ammerman and Cavalli-Sforza found that the spread of farming from the Near East into Europe fits well with the 'wave of advance' model and was possibly characterized by an overall rate of diffusion of approximately one kilometre per year.[5] Neolithic people migrated in search of cultivable lands and in so doing broadcast the basic Neolithic discovery. Migrations occurred because of the turnover, plant, move-on type of primitive agriculture. They may also have occurred because of demographic pressure and 'territoriality'.

The demographic growth that accompanied and followed the Agricultural Revolution usually expressed itself – at least in the first stages – in a multiplication of settlements rather than in the enlargement of the settlement unit. Neolithic Jericho covered an area of about 10 acres, Jarmo an area of about 3 acres, Çatal Hüyük about 32 acres, Djeitum about one acre. In prehistoric Europe, the settlement of Karanovo,

5. Ammerman and Cavalli-Sforza, 1973, pp. 345 ff.

near Stara Zagora in Bulgaria, had about fifty to sixty houses at any one time throughout its history (sixth to second millennium B.C.), so the population would have been about 300. The village of Köln Lindental, south-west of Cologne, possibly had an estimated population of up to 300. The Neolithic village of Barkaer, in Jutland, cannot have included more than 300 or 400 people. The middle Neolithic village on the shores of the Federsee in South Württemberg, Germany, had no more than twenty-five houses, twenty to thirty feet long by about fifteen feet wide.

Later on, in the course of time, with the emergence of higher modes of life, improved productive techniques and organizations, and higher civilizations, population densities increased very noticeably, and towns and large villages appeared – much more extensive than the ancient camps of the early Neolithic peoples. Yet one has to keep in mind that, until the Industrial Revolution, everywhere in the world, towns with more than 100 thousand people remained extremely rare. Big figures are often quoted, but they generally represent gross exaggerations. As late as the sixteenth century, in Europe an average town numbered from 5 to 20 thousand people and any agglomeration with more than 20 thousand inhabitants was considered a big town. Throughout the ages, in any part of the world, the story of agricultural societies remained essentially the story of numerous small, more or less isolated microcosms. Societies were relatively small and families were relatively large; and among other cultural and social factors this relationship explains the role of the family in the agricultural world.

It has been indicated that, on the eve of the Agricultural Revolution, around 10,000 B.C., the human species must have amounted to anything between 2 and 10 million people.

On the eve of the Industrial Revolution, around A.D. 1750, the total world population must have ranged between 650 and

TABLE 17. *Estimates of world population, 1750–1950 (numbers in millions)*

	Area (Km²)	1750	1850	1950
World total	136	750±100	1200±100	2485 (±5%)
Africa	30	100 (?)	100 (?)	217
America	42	15±5	60±10	328
Asia	28	500±50	750±50	1355
Europe	5	120±10	210	392
Oceania	9	2 (?)	2	13
U.S.S.R.	22	30±5	60±5	180

The estimates for 1750 and 1850 are a revised version of the estimates by Willcox and Carr-Saunders. The totals for 1950 are adjusted estimates of the mid-year population as calculated in U.N. *Demographic Yearbook, 1971.*

850 million people. And it is probably correct to say that about 80 per cent of that population was concentrated in Eurasia (see Table 17).

There are a number of reasons that lead us to believe that the total reached in 1750 had never been approached before. The 750 ± 100 million figure is in a way the 'historical' maximum for the agricultural phase of the story of man. The 'theoretical' maximum could have been much higher with better distribution of income, more efficient productive organization, and diffusion of advanced agricultural practices and new kinds of crops into various agricultural areas and into the strongholds of the last Paleolithic hunters (especially in the Americas and Australia). In fact, there are clear indications that the human species was still expanding. Between 1650 and 1750, world population was probably growing at a rate of 0·3–0·4 per cent per year.[6]

6. U.N., 1953, p. 12. For the remarkable growth of Chinese population from 1680 to 1775 see Ping-Ti Ho, 1959, pp. 266–70.

THE INDUSTRIAL REVOLUTION

Then came the Industrial Revolution. And population exploded. Once again, much of the material gain obtained by man in mastering his environment was absorbed by increase in numbers.

The previous chapter illustrated the mechanism of the demographic explosion brought about by the Industrial Revolution. Now, let us assess the result of this explosion. In 1750 the total world population ranged somewhere between 650 and 850 million people. In 1850 it was between 1100 and 1300 million. In 1900 it was around 1600 million. In 1950 it was in the neighbourhood of 2500 million. In 1975 it was over 4000 million, and it is now increasing much faster than ever. The average annual rate of growth was about 0·7 per cent in

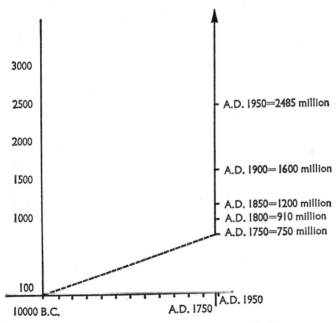

Fig. 11. The growth of world human population

117

1850–1900 and about 1 per cent in 1900–50. It was 1·8 per cent in 1950–60 and about 2 per cent in 1965–70 (see Table 19). Every year there is now a net addition of more than 70 million individuals. A biologist, looking at the diagram showing the recent growth of world population in a long-range perspective (see Fig. 11), said that he had the impression, of being in the presence of the growth curve of a microbe population in a body suddenly struck by some infectious disease. The 'bacillus' man is taking over the world.[7]

EXODUS FROM EUROPE

The demographic explosion did not take place simultaneously all over the globe. It started in Europe – because the Industrial Revolution started there.

Between 1750 and 1950 the population of Europe (including European Russia) grew as follows:[8]

1750 about	145	million
1800 „	187	„
1850 „	265	„
1900 „	400	„
1913 „	468	„
1950 „	550	„

In the meantime, Europe's share of the world population increased from about 21 per cent in 1800 to 22 per cent in 1850 and to at least 25 per cent in 1900. These figures, however, do not tell the entire story. Under the push of internal demo-

7. At a growth rate of 1·5 per cent per annum, the world population, already above 4000 million, will double in 46 years. At a growth rate of 2 per cent per annum it will double in 34 years. Such a rate of population increase as now prevails cannot continue. Even if one is relatively optimistic about actual and potential natural resources of the world and the effect of developments of technology on the production of food and other necessities, it is perfectly obvious that in the not too distant future either the world birth-rate has to go down, or the death-rate has to go up. See Brand, 1959, p. 27.

8. U.N., 1953, p. 11.

graphic pressure and with the advantage of technological superiority – which in one form appeared in superior military power – the Europeans spread all over the world, peacefully and otherwise. They settled in the Americas and Australia. And they came to control Africa and Asia. 'The great exodus from Europe has been the most important migratory movement of the modern era, and perhaps the largest in all human history.'[9]

Today, that expansion still arouses violent emotions around the world. Many peoples fought it fiercely and there is no doubt that European expansion often assumed crude tones of exploitation and oppression. But it is not difficult to maintain that it was less cruel and bloody than most other 'expansions' in human history. There was something epic in a migration that saw Europeans spreading all over the world – building railroads, creating towns and harbours, opening canals, settling desert areas, bringing new lands under cultivation, and building factories, hospitals, missions, and schools.

The number of people who migrated from Europe overseas averaged as follows:[10]

1846–1890	377,000 per year
1891–1920	911,000 „ „
1921–1929	366,000 „ „

On the whole, between 1846 and 1930 over 50 million Europeans sought new homes overseas.[11] The bulk of this emigration was to North America, chiefly to the United States. Of some 20 million persons born in Europe and living in other continents in 1930, nearly 14 million were in North America, about 5 million in Latin America (chiefly Argentina and Brazil), and something more than 1 million in Australia and South Africa.[12]

9. U.N., 1953, p. 98.   10. U.N., 1953, p. 100.
11. Carr-Saunders, 1936, p. 49, and Kirk, 1946, pp. 72–96.
12. U.N., 1953, p. 101.

The growing relative importance of the 'European stock' until the first half of the twentieth century can best be illustrated by the following figures. According to calculations by Professor Kuczynski,[13] the 'white or Caucasian' population of the Earth was nearly 200 million in 1800, and about 700 million in 1930. Total world population was respectively about 910 and 2010 million.[14] This means that the Caucasian population was about 22 per cent of the human species in 1800, and about 35 per cent in 1930.

FEEDING NEW MOUTHS

The diffusion of white people all over the world fostered the diffusion of the Industrial Revolution – just as the migration of early Neolithic farmers had fostered the diffusion of the Agricultural Revolution. The opening of the North-American West, the first cotton mills of Bombay, the first railroads of Argentina and of China, were all phenomena strictly connected with European expansion.

Today the first round of world demographic explosion is over. Europe, North America, and Russia have reached or are reaching the demographic equilibrium of 'industrial' type – with low death- and low birth-rates. We are now facing the second round, which promises to be even more explosive than the first. Asia, South America, and Africa are undergoing a demographic growth of unprecedented magnitude. Their rates of growth range between 2 per cent and 3 per cent per year (see Table 19).

The previous chapter illustrates the mechanism of the demographic explosion of the 'underdeveloped' areas. Here we may consider its implications. The first problem that comes to mind is obviously that of nutrition. In 1961, when this book was originally written, I suggested that the main

13. Kuczynski, 1943, Vol. 12, pp. 240–48.   14. U.N., 1953, p. 11.

economic implications were related to the problem of 'feeding new mouths'. I wrote then: 'An example in point is India. It is estimated that around 1918 India had about 315 million people. The average daily quantity of food grain available to the Indian population was then about 20 ounces *per capita*. By 1945, India's population had increased to about 400 million people. The average daily quantity of food grains available had correspondingly fallen to about 15 ounces *per capita*. After 1945 the situation grew worse and the *per capita* food supply diminished substantially between 1945 and 1952 . . . It is a typical case of a Malthusian trap. Unfortunately it is not the only one. Anyone who has seen poverty and its concomitants in rural areas in China, India or Egypt does not doubt the reality of Malthusian checks, even though he may cavil at Malthusian arithmetic.'

Fifteen years later we have become increasingly aware that the problem of 'feeding new mouths' is not the only, or the most intractable, one. As world population grows, difficulties seem to grow more than proportionately. Medical science and Public Health have accomplished spectacular results over the past one hundred years and possibly this progress has made us exceedingly over-confident about our ability to cope with epidemics. One cannot deny *a priori* the possibility of new types of epidemics whose deadly action might take us by surprise. This is a remote possibility in an orderly industrialized society but it becomes an impending threat in a socially and politically troubled world in which inordinately large numbers of people are crowded into poor and unhealthy environments. Moreover, as industrial production increases, we are impotent witnesses of the growth of output of unwanted by-products which are poisonous to life or impossible to dispose of. Essential raw materials are becoming scarcer and – much worse – we are also beginning to suffer from the shortage of such things as pure air, clean water, and restful

TABLE 18. *World population, 1930–70*

	Area Km² thousands	Estimate of mid-year population (millions)						Birth-rate (‰) 1965–70	Death-rate (‰) 1965–70
		1930	1940	1950	1960	1965	1970		
AFRICA	30,319	164	191	217	270	303	344	46	20
Northern Africa	8525	39	44	51	65	75	78		
Tropical Africa		125	147	166	205	228	257		
AMERICA	42,081	242	274	328	412	460	511	30	10
Northern America	21,515	134	144	166	199	214	228	18	9
Latin America	20,566	108	130	162	213	246	283	39	10
ASIA	27,532	1120	1244	1355	1645	1833	2056	38	15
East Asia	11,757	591	634	657	780	852	930	31	13
South Asia	15,775	529	610	698	865	981	1126	44	16
EUROPE	4936	355	380	392	425	445	462	18	10
OCEANIA	8511	10	11	13	16	18	19	24	10
U.S.S.R.	22,402	179	195	180	214	231	243	18	8
World Total	135,781	2070	2295	2485	2982	3290	3635	34	14

Source: U.N., *Demographic Yearbooks*

silence, things that nobody in the past ever dreamed of considering as economic goods, simply because they were abundantly available to everybody. The concentration of people in the huge megalopolis, which seems to be an inherent and inescapable condition of modern industrialization, is creating social tensions and psychological disturbances of an alarmingly destructive nature: paradoxically our cities are decaying while they are growing in size.

Even if one resists the distressing thought that it is already too late, one can hardly avoid the unpleasant feeling that all we can foresee in the near future is a worsening of the general situation. In order to improve their miserable standards of living, the underdeveloped and developing countries must undergo the Industrial Revolution. If they fail, they are condemned to abject misery. If they succeed, they will add greatly to the problems of pollution and depletion plaguing our planet today.

HOW MANY PEOPLE?

Whether one looks at things from the point of view of human needs or from the point of view of human waste, one has to admit that the immediate future looks problematic.

The argument that there is much empty space left in such inhospitable places as the Sahara Desert or the Brazilian jungle makes no sense economically. It would take huge investments to make life bearable in these places, and the real question is whether it is better to invest huge resources to keep alive – say – another billion people in inhospitable areas of the world, or to use those resources instead to improve the life of the present population.

Notwithstanding the desert and unsettled areas of the Earth, one actually feels that the Industrial Revolution has allowed the human species to increase numerically and to

TABLE 19. *Estimated average annual rates and absolute amounts of natural increase of population, 1960–65 and 1965–70, in major areas and regions of the world*

Areas and regions	Rates, per 1,000		Average annual amounts (millions)	
	1960–65	1965–70	1960–65	1965–70
WORLD TOTAL	19·4	19·8	61·1	68·2
More developed regions	11·5	9·5	11·5	10·0
Less developed regions	23·2	24·5	49·6	58·2
EAST ASIA	17·5	17·5	14·4	15·5
Mainland region	17·8	17·8	12·1	12·9
Japan	9·9	11·0	0·9	1·1
Other East Asia	28·3	25·0	1·4	1·5
SOUTH ASIA	24·8	27·5	23·1	28·6
Middle South Asia	24·5	27·2	15·6	19·1
South-East Asia	25·3	28·1	5·9	7·5
South-West Asia	26·4	28·2	1·6	2·0
EUROPE	8·4	7·8	3·7	3·4
Western Europe	7·2	6·3	1·0	0·9
Southern Europe	11·3	10·1	1·4	1·2
Eastern Europe	8·1	7·8	0·8	0·8
Northern Europe	6·7	6·6	0·5	0·5

SOVIET UNION	15·2	10·2	3·4	2·4
AFRICA	24·1	25·5	7·0	8·3
Western Africa	23·8	24·5	2·2	2·6
Eastern Africa	22·8	24·8	1·8	2·1
Middle Africa	18·9	21·0	0·6	0·7
Northern Africa	28·4	30·0	2·0	2·4
Southern Africa	22·4	23·3	0·4	0·5
NORTHERN AMERICA	13·4	9·8	2·7	2·2
LATIN AMERICA	28·2	28·4	6·6	7·6
Tropical South America	29·6	29·8	3·8	4·3
Middle American Mainland	33·4	33·6	1·7	2·0
Temperate South America	17·5	17·2	0·6	0·7
Caribbean	24·7	24·1	0·5	0·6
OCEANIA	16·9	14·5	0·2	0·6
Australia and New Zealand	13·9	11·5	0·2	0·2
Melanesia	24·2	24·1	0·0	0·2
Polynesia and Micronesia	31·1	30·9	0·0	0·0

Source: United Nations, 1971

extend its control over the environment to a point at which the equilibria on which life rests on this planet are seriously threatened. We easily forget that the economic structure which man has erected rests entirely on the Earth's natural resources and processes. Economic activity depends on the Earth's capacity to supply raw materials, to produce food, and to absorb waste. Without these factors, there would be not even the most rudimentary economic activities on which man's existence depends.

A problem which is, by its very nature, extremely complex, can be put, if one wishes, in rather crude and simple terms. While it took a hundred thousand years for the world's human population to reach 4000 million, it will now take a mere thirty years to add another 4000 million. With the present rate of increase, it can be calculated that in 600 years the number of human beings on the earth will be such that there will be only one square metre for each to live on. It goes without saying that this can never take place. Something will happen to prevent it. But what will happen? To this disturbing question, Malthus's answer was: 'Though we cannot always predict the mode, we may with certainty predict the fact.'

CHAPTER 6

An Age of Transition

IT is a leitmotiv in this book that the three basic types of economic organization – hunting, agricultural, industrial – are accompanied by three corresponding ranges of economic and demographic levels at which human societies operate. The previous chapters were devoted to the assessment of these ranges. Now we have to deal with the notion that the passage of a society from one type of economic organization to another also implies drastic cultural and social changes.

We are in a good position to detect the relevance of such changes, for we ourselves live in an age of transition. Three generations ago more than two-thirds of the people living on the Earth were peasants. In three generations, less than one-third will live 'in the fields'. The Industrial Revolution is spreading all over the world. We witness that the changes are 'not merely industrial but also social and intellectual'.[1] We witness that the technological revolution is accompanied – as Stendhal noticed – by a revolution '*dans les habitudes, les idées, les croyances*'.[2] A new style of life is emerging, as another disappears for ever. We know what is disappearing but we do not know what to expect. This is an age of transition as well as an age of uncertainty and anguish.

Every aspect of life has to be geared to the new modes of production. Family ties are on the wane and give way to broader perspectives for larger social groups. Individual saving gives way to collective social services, undistributed profits, and taxes. The rounded philosophical education of the few is set aside in favour of the technical training of the many. Artistic intuition must give way to technical precision. New juridical institutions, new types of ownership and

1. Ashton, 1950, p. 2.   2. Stendhal, 1925, Vol. 1, p. 91.

management, different distributions of income, new tastes, new values, new ideals have to emerge as an essential part of the industrialization process.

Actually, when 'industrialization' occurs gradually, these socio-cultural changes take place in a balanced process with economic changes. But when, as in many backward areas today, 'industrialization' is artificially speeded up, the socio-cultural environment may show a much greater degree of resistance to change than the economic structure. If such is the case, the static socio-cultural environment can indeed represent a formidable bottleneck and invalidate all efforts to achieve industrialization. This is the reason why some of those societies who want, or are forced, to quicken the pace of industrialization may feel – more or less emotionally – the urge to resort to political and social revolutionary movements. The socio-political revolution is a rough way to break through the socio-cultural bottleneck. All the miseries and the hardships that follow then become part of the price of industrialization.

HOW FAR CAN WE GO?

The people who lived in Western Europe between 1850 and 1913 possibly lived through the golden age of industrialization. The International Exhibitions of London and Paris, the *tour Eiffel* in Paris and the *Mole Antonelliana* in Turin were the expression of the boundless optimism of that age. Imperceptibly at first and then more and more markedly, however, the situation changed. As industrialization progresses, the benefits of additional units of industrial production diminish while their social and economic costs increase. In the developed countries further industrialization is creating all sorts of problems in all aspects of life, in the field of ecology as in that of human relations, in the field of nourishment as in that of education, at the material as well as at the spiritual level. While we strive to deal with one problem we innocently cause another. It is a nightmare and we became aware of it only very recently and almost suddenly. As I mentioned above, one increasingly feels that the Industrial Revolution has allowed the human species to increase numerically and to extend its control over the environment to a point in which the equilibria on which life rests on this planet are seriously threatened. For too long, in the excitement of our progress, we have been blinded by our own inventions. Now we are beginning to ask ourselves how far we can go. It is indicative of this new phase that some people are now advocating a policy of 'zero economic growth'.

'We have not yet been installed for long in this landscape of mines and power stations; we have not long begun to live in this new home which we have not yet finished building. Everything has changed so quickly around us: human relationships, working conditions, customs. Our very psychology has been shaken to its most intimate recesses ...

'We are all of us young barbarians still amazed at our own inventions. To the colonialist the meaning of life is given by conquest. The soldier despises the farmer, but is not the installing of this farmer the aim itself of conquest? In the excitement of our progress we have used men to build railways, raise factories, and bore wells for oil, and have forgotten that we did all this to serve men themselves. During the time of the conquest our morale was a soldier's morale, but now we have to colonize, we have to make this new home, that has not yet acquired a countenance, alive and human. For one generation the problem was to build; for the other the problem is how to live there.'[3]

I mentioned some of the pointers that show the levels which an industrial society may attain. There is no doubt that

3. A. de Saint-Exupéry, 1939, pp. 65–7.

industrialization brings with it an extraordinary improvement in the average material standard of living. It is not to be supposed from all this that the industrial world must necessarily be a good one. There is nothing in the mechanisms of the spread of the Industrial Revolution which guarantees *a priori* that the material result will be used for good ends. Unless mankind makes an enormous effort of self-education the possibility that the Industrial Revolution may eventually come to represent a disastrous calamity for the human race cannot be altogether excluded.

MAN'S BIOLOGICAL PAST

The problem can be considered from another point of view. For more than nine-tenths of its existence, the entire human race has lived in a state of complete savagery. Only very recently, with the discovery of agriculture, has man started on a different course. The events that followed the first Revolution were cumulative. After the supply of biological sources of energy – animals and plants – had been brought under control, other sources were mastered, while the accumulation of knowledge allowed a progressively more efficient exploitation of the newly-conquered energy. The greater the control man acquired over his environment, the greater became his opportunity to extend it.

Ten thousand years may seem a very long span of time, but, from the point of view of the whole history of the earth and mankind, ten thousand years is a very brief fragment. It is truly extraordinary that in about ten thousand years *homo sapiens* has turned himself from a savage into the conqueror not only of this world but also of outer space. This accomplishment actually looks even more remarkable if instead of measuring the time involved by our usual chronological standard – the solar year – we measure it in terms of generations. Considering that the Neolithic Revolution diffused into Europe between 5000 B.C. and 2000 B.C., and assuming for a generation a period of about twenty-five years, slightly more than 150 generations separate each European from his 'nasty and brutish' ancestor.

Here, in fact, lies the great question. Because of a cumulative process, the technical progress of *homo sapiens* has been extremely rapid. Within a relatively small number of generations, man has come to control his environment and to master the most powerful forces of Nature. But how much has he himself improved in quality?

There is no escaping man's origin – a carnivorous and cannibalistic animal – and disgustingly so. Man, the greatest of all scavengers, whether presapient or sapient, could cope with the flesh of any and every competitor – even if it happened to be his own flesh and blood.[4]

A modern optimistic writer, while admitting that 'cannibalism has been a common practice until recently' is emphatic that 'eating your dead enemy or drinking his blood from his empty skull has been a mark of greatest admiration and wish to acquire his virtue. It was a spiritual acknowledgement from the first and in symbolic form survives even in Christian communion.'[5] I fear that there are and always have been very few creatures who would welcome this kind of 'spiritual acknowledgement'. But apart from this, it seems to me that we have to be careful not to confuse the logic of the events. It is not that the crimes of man are bound to have a mark of 'spirituality', but rather that even when man tried to do something 'spiritual', he was bound to show the mark of his origin.

For thousands and thousands of years, for more than nine-tenths of man's existence, the most cruel selective process

4. Dart, 1959, pp. 127–8.   5. Berrill, 1957, p. 85.

progressively worsened the situation, only partially counteracted by the 'good' factor of 'cooperation'. So man evolved – the 'creature fashioned around and selected for hunting . . . the creature whose biological capacities are geared to the life of a hunter'.[6]

The selective process that favoured the success and the multiplication of the aggressive type was certainly not interrupted by the Neolithic Revolution. It continued to operate well into 'civilized' times and to a large extent still operates today, when man can command immensely powerful forces, and his efficiency – for good or for evil – has increased in spectacular fashion. A single man or a small group of individuals – as recent history has dramatically demonstrated – can today bring about unspeakable catastrophes that affect not this or that group, this or that region, but the entire world and the entire human species. As a naturalist, K. Lorenz, once wrote, 'an unprejudiced observer from another planet, looking upon man as he is today, in his hand the atom bomb, the product of his intelligence, in his heart the aggression drive inherited from his anthropoid ancestors, which this same intelligence cannot control, would not prophesy long life for the species. Looking at the situation as a human being whom it personally concerns it seems like a bad dream.'[7]

It is disturbing to see that still today, even in the most advanced countries, in large sections of human society, aggressiveness is praised as a virtue – or at least as a valuable asset – and it is constantly advertised in the motion pictures and on television. We need a crusade against violence and aggressiveness. We need – more than anything else – to educate people to tolerance and gentility. As H. G. Wells once said, the future of mankind depends on the outcome of a race between education and catastrophe. We need to improve the quality of man.

6. Coon, 1958, pp. 8 and 212.   7. Lorenz, 1966, p. 49.

132

QUALITY OR QUANTITY?

Improvement in quality of the human species is not necessarily alternative to a growth in quantity. A larger population may mean greater possibilities in the division of labour and economies of scale. These possibilities may contribute to the growth of *per capita* income, to better levels of living, and to better education. But beyond certain points, quantity and quality may well become competitive. At the end of the eighteenth century, in the course of a journey through China as a private secretary to the Earl of Macartney, ambassador from the King of England, John Barrow witnessed a peculiar scene:

Of the number of persons who had crowded down to the banks of the grand canal [to Canton], several had posted themselves upon the high projecting stern of an old vessel which, unfortunately, breaking down with the weight, the whole group tumbled with the wreck into the canal. Although numbers of boats were sailing about the place, none were perceived to go to the assistance of those that were struggling in the water; one fellow was observed very busily employed in picking up, with his boat-hook, the hat of a drowning man.[8]

This happened because men were over-abundant and hats were scarce. If hats had been over-abundant and men scarce, the story would have been totally different. It is tragically inevitable that, as human beings become over-abundant in relation to other resources, their marginal value diminishes and the dignity of human life deteriorates correspondingly. For the safeguard of the worth and sanctity of human life it is imperative that man does not become the cheapest of all commodities.

The question whether the allocation of available resources between quantity and quality has been on the whole well done in the history of mankind, is impossible to answer. Among

8. Barrow, 1805, p. 112.

133

other things it implies the objectively impossible assessment of all kinds of ethical and cultural values and standards. Some facts, though, may perhaps help to give at least a general idea about what the general tendency has been. When the Neolithic Revolution occurred about ten thousand years ago, there were – as we have seen – fewer than 10 million people on the Earth. In A.D. 1950 there were almost 2,500 million. Now, of the adult portion of this population, about 50 per cent were totally illiterate (see Table 20). A mere glance at these figures immediately suggests that far too much of the available resources was used up by the quantitative increase of mankind at the expense of its qualitative improvement.

We must invest more of our resources in the qualitative improvement of man. As Julian Huxley once said, we must place meaningful quality above meaningless quantity. There must be a combined effort in both the public and the private sectors toward such a goal. In this regard it should be remembered that what is needed is not merely more technical knowledge. What man today desperately needs is the kind of education that allows him to make wise use of the techniques he possesses. 'We live at a time when man, Lord of all things, is not Lord of himself. He feels lost amid his own abundance ... To modern man is happening what was said of the Regent during the minority of Louis XV: he had all the talents except the talent to make use of them.'[9]

A well-known and reputable economist recently wrote that 'we do not know what the purpose of life is, but if it were happiness, then evolution could just as well have stopped a long time ago, since there is no reason to believe that men are happier than pigs or than fishes. What distinguishes men from pigs is that men have greater control over their environment, not that they are more happy. And on this test, economic growth is greatly to be desired.'[10] The basic

9. Ortega y Gasset, 1932, p. 47.   10. Lewis, 1955, p. 421.

TABLE 20. *Estimated adult literacy rates in the world population, 1950*

	Estimated population 15 years old and over (millions)	Estimated adult literacy rates (per cent)
WORLD	1587	55–57
AFRICA		
North Africa	40	10–15
Tropical and South	80	15–20
AMERICA		
North America	126	96–97
Middle America	30	58–60
South America	67	56–58
ASIA		
South West	37	20–25
South Central	287	15–20
South East	102	30–35
East	404	50–55
EUROPE		
North & West	102	98–99
Central	96	97–98
South	95	79–80
U.S.S.R.	112	89–90
OCEANIA	9	90–95

See UNESCO, 1957, p. 15, and Cipolla, 1969.

criticism of such a piece of logic was written centuries ago by Plato (*Eutidemos,* XI): 'Wealth is not a blessing in itself; if directed by ignorance wealth is a greater evil than poverty because it can push things more strongly than poverty in the wrong direction; if directed by wisdom and knowledge, wealth is a blessing.' 'Control over environment' may be used as it was used at Coventry and Hiroshima. If this is the purpose of human life, then I, for myself, would rather be a pig. We do not know what human happiness is. But we know what it is not. We know that human happiness cannot thrive

135

where intolerance and brutality prevail. There is nothing more dangerous than technical knowledge when unaccompanied by respect for human life and human values. The introduction of modern techniques in environments that are still dominated by intolerance and aggressiveness is a most alarming development. As I wrote elsewhere, 'Instructing a savage in advanced techniques does not change him into a civilized person; it just makes him an efficient savage.'[11] Ethical progress has to accompany technical and economic development. While teaching techniques, we have to teach also respect for the dignity and worth and indeed the sanctity of human personality. Urgent action is needed lest the last state turn out to be worse than the first.

11. Cipolla, 1969, p. 110.

Bibliography

ACSÁDI, G., and NEMESKÉRI, J., 1970. *History of Human Lifespan and Mortality.* Budapest.

ALSBERG, C., 1948. *Chemistry and the Theory of Population.* Stanford, California.

AMAR, J. 1920. *The Human Motor.* London.

AMMERMAN, A. J., and CAVALLI-SFORZA, L. L., 1973. 'A Population Model for the diffusion of early farming in Europe', *The Explanation of Culture Change* (ed. C. Renfrew). London.

ANGEL, J. L., 1971. 'Early Neolithic Skeletons from Çatal Hüyük', *Anatolian Studies,* 21.

1971. *The People of Lerna.* Princeton.

ARMENGAUD, A., DUPAQUIER, J., and REINHARD, M., 1968. *Histoire Générale de la Population Mondiale.* Paris.

ASHTON, T. S., 1950. *The Industrial Revolution.* London.

AUKRUST, O., 1959. 'Investment and Economic Growth', *Productivity Measurement Review,* 16.

AYRES, E., and SCARLOTT, C. A., 1952. *Energy Sources.* New York, Toronto, London.

BAILLOUD, G., 1955. *Les Civilisations néolithiques de la France dans leur contexte européen.* Paris.

BAIROCH, P., 1971. 'Structure de la population active mondiale de 1700 à 1970', *Annales: Économies, Sociétés, Civilisations,* 26.

BAIROCH, P., et al., 1968. *International Historical Statistics.* Brussels.

BAIROCH, P., and LIMBOR, J. M., 1968. 'Changes in the Industrial Distribution of the World Labour Force', *Inter. Labour Rev.,* 98.

BALDWIN, R. E., 1958. 'The commodity composition of trade', *The Review of Economics and Statistics,* 40.

BANKS, A. L., 1955. 'The Relationship between Disease Control and Changes in Population Growth and Age Structure', *The Numbers of Man and Animals* (ed. J. B. Cragg and N. W. Pirie). Edinburgh and London.

BARNETT, R. D., 1958. 'Early Shipping in the Near East', *Antiquity,* 32.

BARROW, J., 1805. *Travels in China.* Philadelphia.

BARTHOLOMEW, G. A., and BIRDSELL, J. B., 1953. 'Ecology and the Protohominids', *American Anthropologist,* 55.

BATES, M., 1953. 'Human ecology', *Anthropology Today* (ed. A. L. Kroeber). Chicago.

1955. *The Prevalence of People*. New York.

BAUER, P. T., and YAMEY, B. S., 1951. 'Economic Progress and Occupational Distribution', *Economic Journal*, 61.

BAUM, V. A., 1955. 'Prospects for the Application of Solar Energy and some Research Results in the U.S.S.R.', *Proceedings of the World Symposium on Applied Solar Energy*. Phoenix, Arizona.

BAUTIER, A. M., 1960. 'Les plus anciennes mentions de moulins hydrauliques industriels et de moulins à vent', *Bulletin Philologique et Historique*, 2.

BECKER, C. J., 1955. 'The Introduction of Farming into Northern Europe', *Cahiers d'histoire mondiale*, 2.

BEFU, H., and CHARD, C. S., 1960. 'Preceramic Cultures in Japan', *American Anthropologist*, 62.

BELLIDO, A. G., 1955. 'La vida media en la España romana', *Revista intern. de sociología*, 13.

BELSHAW, H., 1956. *Population Growth and Levels of Consumption*. London.

BENNETT, M. K., 1951. 'International Disparities in Consumption Levels', *American Economic Review*, 41.

BERGSON, A., 1961. *The Real National Income of Soviet Russia since 1928*. Cambridge, Mass.

BERRILL, N. J., 1957. *Man's Emerging Mind*. New York.

BHATTACHARJEE, J. P., and associates, 1958. 'Trend of Consumption of Food and Foodgrains in India', *Tenth International Conference of Agricultural Economists* (ed. J. P. Bhattacharjee). Bombay.

BIRD, J. B., 1948. 'Pre-ceramic Cultures in Chicama and Viru', *American Antiquity*, 13, 4, Part II.

BIREMBAUT, A., 1959. 'L'industrie du pétrole au XIX siècle', *Cahiers d'histoire mondiale*, 5.

BISHOP, C. W., 1933. 'The Neolithic Age in Northern China', *Antiquity*, 7.

BLOCH, M., 1935. 'Avènement et conquêtes du moulin à eau', *Annales d'histoire économique et sociale*, 7.

1935. 'Les Inventions médiévales', *Annales d'histoire économique et sociale*, 7.

BOAS, M., 1962. *The Scientific Renaissance*. New York.

BORAZ, J., 1959. 'First Tools in Mankind', *Natural History*.

BOULDING, K. E., 1970. *Economics as a Science*. New York.

BOURGEOIS-PICHAT, Y., 1951. 'Evolution générale de la population française depuis le XVIII siècle', *Population*, 6.

BOWEN, W. G., 1963. 'Assessing the economic contribution of education: an appraisal of alternative approaches', in *Higher Education. Report of the Committee under the Chairmanship of Lord Robbins*. London.

BRAIDWOOD, R. J., 1961. *Prehistoric Man*. Chicago.

BRAIDWOOD, R. J., and REED, C. A., 1957. 'The Achievement and Early Consequences of Food Production', Cold Spring Harbor Symposia on Quantitative Biology, Vol. 22, *Population Studies: Animal Ecology and Demography*. New York.

BRAIDWOOD, R. J., and WILLEY, G. R. (eds.), 1962. *Courses toward Urban Life* (Viking Fund Publications in Anthropology, No. 32). Chicago.

BRAND, W., 1959. 'The World Population Problem', *International Population Conference*. Vienna.

BRØNDSTED, J., 1960. *The Vikings*. Harmondsworth.

BROTHWELL, D., and SANDISON, A. T., 1967. *Diseases in Antiquity*. Springfield.

BROWN, H., 1954. *The Challenge of Man's Future*. New York.

BURDFORD, A., 1960. 'Heavy Transport in Classical Antiquity', *Economic History Review*, 13.

BURKITT, M., 1956. *The Old Stone Age*. New York.

BURN, A. R., 1953. 'Hic breve vivitur. A study of the Expectation of Life in the Roman Empire', *Past and Present*, 4.

BUTTERFIELD, H., 1962. *The Origins of Modern Science*. New York.

CARDAN, J., 1962. *The Book of My Life* (transl. and edited by J. Stoner). New York.

CARLSON, A. J., 1955. 'Science versus life', *Journal of the American Medical Association*, 157.

CARR-SAUNDERS, A. M., 1936. *World Population*. Oxford.

CARUS-WILSON, E. M., 1941. 'An Industrial Revolution of the Thirteenth Century', *Economic History Review*, 11.

C.E.C.A., 1957. *Studio sulla struttura e tendenze dell'economia energetica nei paesi della Comunità*. Luxembourg.

1957 (2). *Un secolo di sviluppo della produzione dell'acciaio*. Luxembourg.

CHANDRASEKKAR, S., 1959. *Infant Mortality in India*. London.

CHANG, KWANG-CHIH, 1963. *The Archaeology of Ancient China*. New Haven.

1967. 'The Yale Expedition to Taiwan and the Southeast Asian Horticultural Evolution', *Discovery*, 2.

CHASTELAND, J. C., 1960. 'Evolution générale de la mortalité en Europe Occidentale de 1900 à 1950'. *Population*, 15.

CIPOLLA, C. M., 1965. 'Four centuries of Italian demographic development', in D. V. Glass and D. E. C. Eversley (eds.), *Population in History*. London.

1967. *Clocks and Culture*. London.

1969. *Literacy and Development in the West*. Harmondsworth.

CLARK, C., 1957. *The Conditions of Economic Progress*. London.

CLARK, G., 1969. *World Prehistory*. Cambridge.

CLARK, G., and PIGGOTT, S., 1965. *Prehistoric Societies*. London.

CLARK, J. D., 1959. *The Prehistory of Southern Africa*. London.

CLARK, J. G. D., 1952. *Prehistoric Europe, the Economic Basis*. London.

CLARK, J. G. D., and GODWIN, H., 1962. 'The Neolithic in the Cambridgeshire Fens'. *Antiquity*, 36.

COALE, A. J., 1959. 'Increases in Expectation of Life and Population Growth', *International Population Conference*. Vienna.

1965. 'Population and Economic Development', in P. M. Hauser (ed.), *The Population Dilemma*. Englewood Cliffs, N.J.

COALE, A. J., and HOOVER, E. M., 1958. *Population Growth and Economic Development in Low-Income Countries*. Princeton.

COLE, S., 1954. *The Prehistory of East Africa*. Harmondsworth.

1965. *The Neolithic Revolution*. London.

COLLVER, O. A., 1965. *Birth Rates in Latin America*. Berkeley, California.

COON, C. S., 1957. *The Seven Caves*. New York.

1958. *The Story of Man*. New York.

COONTZ, S. H., 1957. *Population Theories and their Economic Interpretation*. London.

COTTRELL, F., 1955. *Energy and Society*. New York, Toronto, London.

DART, R. A., 1959. *Adventures with the Missing Link*. New York.

DARWIN, C. G., 1953. *The Next Million Years*. New York.

DAVIES, R. E. G., 1954. *A History of the World Airlines*. New York, Toronto.

DAVIS, K., 1951. 'Population and the Further Spread of Industrial Society', *Proceedings of the American Philosophical Society*, 95.

1956. 'The Amazing Decline of Mortality in Underdeveloped Areas', *American Economic Review*, 46.

DAVIS, K., and BLAKE, J., 1956. 'Social Structure and Fertility: an

142

Analytic Framework', *Economic Development and Cultural Change*, 4.

DEANE, P., 1967. *The First Industrial Revolution*. Cambridge.

DEEVEY, E. S., 1960. 'The Human Population', *Scientific American*.

DERRY, T. K., and WILLIAMS T. I., 1960. *A Short History of Technology*. Oxford.

DEWHURST, J. F. (ed.), 1955. *America's Needs and Resources*. New York.

1961. *Europe's Needs and Resources*. New York, London.

DIJKSTERHUIS, E. J., 1961. *The Mechanisation of the World Picture*. Oxford.

DRACHMANN, A. G., 1963. *The Mechanical Technology of Greek and Roman Antiquity*. Copenhagen, Madison, London.

DUBLIN, L. I., LOTKA, A. J., and SPIEGELMAN, M., 1949. *Length of Life: A Study of the Life Table*. New York.

DURAND, J. D., 1958. 'World Population: Trends and Prospects', *Population and World Politics* by P. M. Hauser. Glencoe, Ill.

EDEL, M., 1973. *Economics and the Environment*. Englewood Cliffs, N.J.

FABRICANT, S., 1958. *Basic Facts on Productivity Change*. National Bureau of Economic Research, Occasional Paper, 63. New York.

FAIRSERVIS, W. A., 1956. 'Excavations in the Quetta Valley, West Pakistan', *Anthropological Papers of the American Museum of Natural History*, 45, Part 2. New York.

1959. *The Origin of Oriental Civilization*. New York.

FEBVAY, M., and CROZE, M., 1954. 'Nouvelles données sur la mortalité infantile', *Population*, 9.

FLINN, M. W., 1970. *British Population Growth 1700–1850*. London.

FORBES, R. J., 1958. *Man, the Maker*. London, New York.

FORD FOUNDATION, 1959. *India's Food Crisis*. Delhi.

FORDE, C. D., 1955. *Habitat, Economy and Society*. London.

FOURASTIÉ, J., 1949. *Le Grand Espoir du XX siècle*. Paris.

FRANKFORT, H., 1951. *The Birth of Civilization in the Near East*. London.

GALLAGHER, L. J. (ed.), 1953. *The Journals of Matthew Ricci*. New York.

GENICOT, L., 1953. 'Sur les témoignages d'accroissement de la population en Occident du XI au XIII siècle'. *Cahiers d'histoire mondiale*, 1 (transl. and reproduced in S. L. Thrupp, *Change in Medieval Society*. New York, 1954).

GILBERT, M., and associates, 1958. *Comparative National Products and Price Levels*. Paris.

GILLE, B., 1954. 'Le Moulin à eau, une révolution technique mediévale', *Techniques et civilisations*, 3.

1956. 'Les développements technologiques en Europe de 1100 à 1400', *Cahiers d'histoire mondiale*, 3.

GINSBURG, N., 1961. *Atlas of Economic Development*. Chicago.

GLASS, D. V., and EVERSLEY, D. E. C. (eds.), 1965. *Population in History*. London.

GLOB, P. V., 1949. 'Barkaer, Danmarks aeldste landsby', *Fra Nationalmuseets*, Arbejdsmark.

GORDON CHILDE, V., 1955. *Man Makes Himself*. New York.

1958. *The Prehistory of European Society*. Harmondwsorth.

GOSH, D., 1946. *Pressure of Population and Economic Efficiency in India*. Oxford.

GOUBERT, P., 1960. *Beauvais et le Beauvaisis de 1600 à 1730*. Paris.

GREGG, A., 1955. 'Hidden Hunger at the Summit', *Population Bulletin*, 11.

HAJNAL, J., 1965. 'European marriage patterns in perspective', in D. V. Glass and D. E. C. Eversley (eds.), *Population in History*. London.

HALL, A. R., 1954. *The Scientific Revolution*. London, New York.

HARDIN, G., 1968. 'The Tragedy of the Commons', *Science*, 162.

HARE, R., 1954. *Pomp and Pestilence*. London.

HARLAN, J. R., 1971. 'Agricultural Origins: centers and non centers', *Science*, 174.

HART, I. B., 1961. *James Watt and the History of Steam Power*. New York.

HARTLEY, H., 1950. 'Man's Use of Energy', *The Advancement of Science*, 7.

HARTWELL, R. M. (ed.), 1967. *The Causes of the Industrial Revolution*. London.

HAUDRICOURT, A. G., 1936. 'De l'origine de l'attelage moderne', *Annales d'histoire économique et sociale*, 8.

HAUSER, P. M. (ed.), 1965. *The Population Dilemma*. Englewood Cliffs, N.J.

HAWKES, J., and WOOLLEY, L., 1963. *Prehistory and the Beginnings of Civilization*. New York and Evaston.

HEICHELHEIM, F. M., 1956. 'Man's Role in Changing the Face of the Earth in Classical Antiquity', *Kyklos*, 9.

1958. *An Ancient Economic History*. Leiden.

HELLEINER, K. F., 1957. 'The Vital Revolution Reconsidered', *Canadian Journal of Economics and Political Science*, 23.

HENRY, L., 1957. 'La Mortalité d'après les inscriptions funéraires', *Population*, 12.

1959. L'Âge du décès d'après les inscriptions funéraires', *Population*, 14.

HICKS, J., 1969. *A Theory of Economic History*. Oxford.

HO, P. T., 1969. 'The Loess and the Origin of Chinese Agriculture', *American Historical Review*, 75.

HOLMBERG, L., 1962. 'Mauritius, a Study in Disaster', *Economy and History*, 5.

HOWELLS, W., 1954. *Back of History*. New York.

1959. *Mankind in the Making*. New York.

HUBBERT, M. K., 1971. 'The Energy Resources of the Earth', in *Energy and Power* (a *Scientific American* book). San Francisco.

HUGHES, C. (ed.), 1903. *Moryson's Itinerary*. London.

HUXLEY, A., 1958. *Brave New World Revisited*. New York.

1964. *Tomorrow and tomorrow and tomorrow*. New York.

HUXLEY, J., 1957. *New Bottles for New Wine*. New York.

IHDE, A. J., 1958. 'Chemical Industry 1780–1900', *Cahiers d'histoire mondiale*, 4.

I.L.O., 1956. 'La Population active dans le monde: répartition par secteurs économiques', *Revue internationale du travail*, 73.

IMLAH, A. H., 1958. *Economic Elements in the Pax Britannica*. Cambridge, Mass.

IVERSEN, J., 1941. 'Land Occupation in Denmark's Stone Age', *Danmarks Geologiske Undersogelse*, 66.

JONES, R. F., 1961. *Ancients and Moderns*. St Louis.

KANTNER, J. F., 1960. 'Recent Demographic trends in the U.S.S.R.', *Population Trends in Eastern Europe, the U.S.S.R. and Mainland China*. New York.

KAPADIA, K. M., 1958. *Marriage and Family in India*. London, Calcutta.

KENDRICK, J. W., 1956. *Productivity Trends: Capital and Labor*. National Bureau of Economic Research, Occasional Paper, 53. New York.

KENYON, K. M., 1957. 'Reply to Professor Braidwood', *Antiquity*, 31.

1959. 'Earliest Jericho', *Antiquity*, 33.

1960. *Archaeology in the Holy Land*. London.

KEYFITZ, N., and FLIEGER, W., 1971. *Population*. San Francisco.

KEYS, A., 1958. 'Minimum Subsistence', *The Population Ahead* (ed. R. G. Francis). Minneapolis.

145

KIRK, D., 1946. *Europe's Population in the Interwar Years.* League of Nations.

KNEESE, A. V., AYERS, R. U., D'ARGE, R. C., 1970. *Economics and the Environment.* Washington, D.C.

KROEBER, A. L., 1948. 'Summary and Interpretations', in 'A Reappraisal of Peruvian Archaeology' (ed. W. C. Bennett), *American Antiquity*, 13, 4, Part II.

KRZYWICKI, L., 1934. *Primitive Society and its Vital Statistics.* London.

KUCZYNSKI, R. R., 1943. 'Population', *Encyclopaedia of Social Sciences.*

KUZNETS, S., 1946. *National Income, a Summary of Findings.* New York.

1952. 'Long Term Changes in the National Income of the United States of America since 1870', *Income and Wealth*, series 2. Cambridge.

1956. 'Quantitative Aspects of the Economic Growth of Nations', *Economic Development and Cultural Change*, 5.

1959. *Economic Growth.* Glencoe, Ill.

LANDES, D. S., 1969. *The Unbound Prometheus.* Cambridge.

LAVE, L. B., 1966. *Technological Change.* Englewood Cliffs, N. J.

LE BARON BOWEN, R., 1960. 'Egypt's earliest sailing ships', *Antiquity*, 34.

LEFEBVRE DES NOÈTTES, R., 1931. *L'Attelage et le cheval de selle à travers les âges.* Paris.

LEWIS, W. A., 1955. *The Theory of Economic Growth.* London.

LORENZ, K., 1966. *On Aggression.* London.

LORIMER, F., 1954. *Culture and Human Fertility.* Paris.

MACKENROTH, G., 1953. *Bevölkerungslehre.* Berlin.

MACNEISH, R. S., 1961. *Annual Reports of the Tehuacan Archaeological-Botanical Project.* Andover, Mass.

1964. *El origen de la civilización mesoamericana.* Mexico.

1965. 'The Origins of American Agriculture,' *Antiquity*, 39.

MAJUMDAR, R. C., 1951. *The History and Culture of the Indian People.* London.

MANGELSDORF, P. G., 1954. 'New Evidence on the Origin and Ancestry of Maize', *American Antiquity*, 19.

MANTOUX, P., 1928. *The Industrial Revolution in the Eighteenth Century.* London.

MASON, J. ALDEN, 1957. *The Ancient Civilizations of Peru.* Harmondsworth.

146

BIBLIOGRAPHY

MASSON, W. M., 1961. 'The first farmers in Turkmenia', *Antiquity*, 35.
MATHER, K. M., 1944. *Enough and to Spare*. New York.
MATHIAS, P., 1969. *The First Industrial Nation*. London.
MELLAART, J., 1964. 'Excavations at Çatal Hüyük', *Anatolian Studies*, 14.
1965. *Earliest Civilizations of the Near East*. London.
1967. *Çatal Hüyük*. London.
MINKES, A. L., 1955. 'Statistical Evidence and the Concept of Tertiary Industry', *Economic Development and Cultural Change*, 3.
MITCHELL, B. R., and DEANE, P. H., 1962. *Historical Statistics*. Cambridge.
MOLS, R., 1955. *Introduction à la démographie historique des villes d'Europe du XIV au XVIII siècle*. Louvain.
MORITZ, L. A., 1958. *Grain Mills and Flour in Classical Antiquity*. Oxford.
MULLETT, C. F., 1956. *The Bubonic Plague and England*. Lexington, Kentucky.
MURRAY, J., 1970. *The First European Agriculture: a study of the osteological and botanical evidence*. Edinburgh.
NEEDHAM, J., 1954–. *Science and Civilization in China*. Cambridge.
NEF, J. U., 1965. *The Conquest of the Material World*. Chicago.
NEUSTUPNY, E., 1968. 'Chronology of the Neolithic and Aeneolithic Periods', *Slovenska Archaelogia*, 16.
NOUGIER, L. R., 1950. *Les Civilisations campigniennes en Europe Occidentale*. Le Mans.
OAKLEY, K., 1955. 'Fire as Paleolithic Tool and Weapon', *Proceedings of the Prehistoric Society*, 21.
1956. 'The Earliest Fire Makers', *Antiquity*, 30.
OLIVIER, M., 1935. *Dix ans de politique sociale à Madagascar*. Paris.
O.N.U., 1956. 'Besoin du monde en énergie en 1975 et en l'an 2000', *Actes de la conférence internationale sur l'utilisation de l'énergie atomique à des fins pratiques*. Geneva.
ORTEGA Y GASSET, J., 1932. *The Revolt of the Masses*. New York.
OSTWALD, W., 1909. *Energetische Grundlagen der Kulturwissenschaft*. Leipzig.
PANIKKAR, K. M., 1959. *Asia and Western Dominance*. London.
PARETTI, V., and BLOCH, G., 1956. 'Industrial Production in Western Europe and the United States 1901 to 1955', *Banca Nazionale del Lavoro, Quarterly Review*, 39.
PASSMORE, R., 1962. 'Estimation of Food Requirements', *Journal of the Royal Statistical Society*, series A, vol. 125.

147

PATEL, S. J., 1961. 'Rates of Industrial Growth in the Last Century, 1860–1958', *Economic Development and Cultural Change*, Vol. 9, No. 3.

PEARL, R., 1925. *The Biology of Population Growth*. New York.

P.E.P. (ed.), 1956. *World Population and Resources*. London.

PHILLIPSON, J., 1969. *Ecological Energetics*. London.

PIGGOTT, S., 1950. *Prehistoric India*. London.

1954. *The Neolithic Cultures of the British Isles*. Cambridge.

1965. *Ancient Europe from the beginnings of Agriculture to Classical Antiquity*. Edinburgh.

PING-TI HO, 1959. *Studies on the Population of China*. Cambridge, Mass.

PIRENNE, J., 1950. *Les Grands Courants de l'histoire universelle*. Paris.

PIRIE, N. W., 1962. 'Future Sources of Food Supply', *Journal of the Royal Statistical Society*, series A, vol. 125.

PRESSAT, R., 1972. *Demographic Analysis*. Chicago – New York.

PUTNAM, P. C., 1950. *The Future of Land Based on Nuclear Fuels*. Oak Ridge.

1953. *Energy in the Future*. New York.

PYKE, M., 1950. *Industrial Nutrition*. London.

QUITTA, H., 1967. 'The C14 Chronology of the Central and S.E. European Neolithic', *Antiquity*, 41.

RATZEL, F., 1891. *Anthropogeographie*. Stuttgart.

REDDAWAY, W. B., 1962. *The Development of the Indian Economy*. London.

RUSSELL, J. C., 1958. 'Late Ancient and Medieval Population', *Transactions of the American Philosophical Society*, N.S., 48, III.

SAINT-EXUPÉRY, A. DE, 1939. *Terre des hommes*. Paris.

SANKALIA, H. D., 1963. *Prehistory and Protohistory in India and Pakistan*. Bombay.

SARKAN, N. K., 1957. *The Demography of Ceylon*. Ceylon.

SAUER, C. O., 1952. *Agricultural Origins and Dispersal*. New York.

SAUVY, A., 1958. *De Malthus à Mao Tse-Tung*. Paris.

SCHELLING, T. C., 1971. 'On the Ecology of Micromotives', *The Public Interest*, 25.

SCHULTZ, T. W., 1963. *The Economic Value of Education*. New York and London.

SCHURR, S. H., and NETSCHERT, B. C., 1960. *Energy in the American Economy*. Baltimore.

SLICHER VAN BATH, B. H., 1963. 'Yield ratios, 810–1820', *A. A. G. Bijdragen* 10.

SPENGLER, J. J., 1956. 'Basic data on economic development', *Population Theory and Policy* (ed. J. J. Spengler and O. D. Duncan). Glencoe, Ill.

SRUEVER, S. (ed.), 1971. *Prehistoric Agriculture.* Garden City, N.Y.

STARR, C., 1971. 'Energy and Power', *Energy and Power*. A *Scientific American* Book. San Francisco.

STEARNS, R. P., 1943. 'The Scientific Spirit in England in early modern times', *Isis*, 96.

STENDHAL, 1925. *Racine et Shakespeare.* Paris.

STOLNITZ, G. J., 1954–5. 'A Century of International Mortality Trends', *Population Studies*, 8.

TACHEN, 1946. *Population in Modern China.* Chicago.

TAEUBER, J. B., 1956. 'Population Growth in South East Asia', *Demographic Analysis* (ed. J. J. Spengler and O. D. Duncan). Glencoe, Ill.

TAYLOR, K. W., 1956. 'Some Aspects of Population History', *Demographic Analysis* (ed. J. J. Spengler and O. D. Duncan). Glencoe, Ill.

THIRRING, H., 1958. *Energy for Man.* Bloomington, Indiana.

TINBERGEN, J., 1942. 'Zur Theorie der langfristigen Wirtschaftsentwicklung', *Weltwirtschaftliche Archiv*, 55.

TOYNBEE, A. J., 1960. 'Education: The Long View', *Saturday Review*.

TS. S. U. S.S.S.R., 1962. *Narodnoe Khoziaistvo SSSR v 1961 g.* Moscow.

UCKO, P. J., and DIMBLEBY, G. W. (eds.), 1969. *The Domestication and Exploitation of Plants and Animals.* London.

U.N., 1953. *The Determinants and Consequences of Population Trends.* New York.

1958. *Recent Trends in Fertility in Industrialized Countries.* New York.

1971. *The World Population Situation in 1970.* New York.

UNESCO, 1957. *World Illiteracy at Mid-century.* Paris.

URLANIS, T. S., 1941. *Rost naselenija v Evropi.* Moscow.

1963. *Rozhdaemost' i prodolzhitelnost' zhizni v S.S.S.R.* Moscow.

U.S. BUREAU OF CENSUS, 1960. *Historical Statistics of the U.S.* Washington, D.C.

USHER, A. P., 1959. *A History of Mechanical Inventions.* Boston, Mass.

VAIZEY, J., 1962. *The Economics of Education.* London.

VALLOIS, H. V., 1937. 'La durée de la vie chez l'homme fossile', *Anthropologie*, 47.

1960. 'Vital Estimates in Prehistoric Population as Determined from Archaeological Data', *The Application of Quantitative Methods in Archaeology*, R. F. Heizer and S. F. Cook (eds.), New York.

VAN NORT, L., and KARON, B. P., 1955. 'Demographic Transition re-examined', *The American Sociological Review*, 20.

VARAGNAC, A. (ed.), 1959. *L'Homme avant l'écriture*. Paris.

WEIDENREICH, F., 1949. 'The duration of life of fossil man in China and the pathological lesions found in his skeleton', *The Shorter Anthropological Papers of Franz Weidenreich*. New York.

WHEELER, R. E. M., 1968. *The Indus Civilization*. Cambridge.

WHITE, L. A., 1954. 'The Energy Theory of Cultural Development', *Professor Ghurye Felicitation Volume*, ed. K. M. Kapadia. Bombay.

WHITE, L. T., 1940. 'Technology and Invention in the Middle Ages', *Speculum*, 15.

WILLCOX, W. F., 1940. *Studies in American Demography*. Ithaca, N.Y.

WILSON, G. B. L., 1960. 'Technical Gains during the Nineteenth Century', *Cahiers d'histoire mondiale*, 6.

WOLFE, A. B., 1933. 'The Fecundity and Fertility of Early Man', *Human Biology*.

WOOLLEY, C. L., 1929. *The Sumerians*. Oxford.

WOYTINSKY, W. S., and WOYTINSKY, E. S., 1955. *World Commerce and Governments*. New York.

WRIGLEY, E. A., 1962. 'The Supply of Raw Materials in the Industrial Revolution', *The Economic History Review*, ser. 2, vol. 15.

1969. *Population and History*. New York, Toronto.

ZEUNER, F. E., 1956. 'The Radiocarbon Age of Jericho', *Antiquity*, 30.

1958. *Dating the Past*. London.

1963. *A History of Domesticated Animals*. London.

ZIMMERMANN, E. W., 1951. *World Resources and Industries*. New York.

Index

153

The Economic History of World Population

CARLO M. CIPOLLA

This book presents a global view of the demographic and economic development of mankind.

Professor Cipolla has deliberately adopted a new point of view and has tried to trace the history of the great trends in population and wealth which have affected mankind as a whole. For it would have been inadequate to regard such a global history as being merely the sum total of national economic histories in abridged form. Among the massive problems that face the human race the author emphasizes the demographic explosion, the economic backwardness of vast areas, the spread of industrial revolution and of technical knowledge. Whilst the theoretical approach can help our analysis of these problems, Professor Cipolla believes that they can only be wholly grasped and solved when they are studied in their full historical perspective.